Better Homes and Gardens®

CHRISTMAS
FROM THE HEART®

Volume 20

Meredith® Consumer Marketing
Des Moines, Iowa

Better Homes and Gardens®

CHRISTMAS
FROM THE HEART®

Meredith Corporation Consumer Marketing
Senior Vice President, Consumer Marketing: David Ball
Consumer Product Marketing Director: Steve Swanson
Consumer Product Marketing Manager: Wendy Merical
Business Director: Ron Clingman
Photographers: Scott Little, Kritsada Panichgul, Jay Wilde

Waterbury Publications, Inc.
Contributing Editor: Carol Field Dahlstrom
Contributing Graphic Designer: Angie Haupert Hoogensen
Contributing Illustrator: Chris Neubauer Graphics
Contributing Food Editor: Lois White
Contributing Food Stylists: Charles Worthington, Jennifer Peterson
Contributing Copy Editor: Peg Smith
Contributing Proofreaders: Terri Fredrickson,
Gretchen Kauffman

Editorial Director: Lisa Kingsley
Creative Director: Ken Carlson
Associate Editors: Tricia Laning, Mary Williams
Associate Design Directors: Doug Samuelson, Bruce Yang
Production Assistant: Mindy Samuelson

***Better Homes and Gardens*® Magazine**
Editor in Chief: Gayle Goodson Butler
Art Director: Michael D. Belknap
Deputy Editor, Food and Entertaining: Nancy Wall Hopkins
Senior Food Editor: Richard Swearinger
Associate Food Editor: Erin Simpson
Editorial Assistant: Renee Irey

Meredith Publishing Group
Executive Vice President: Andy Sareyan
Vice President, Manufacturing: Bruce Heston

Meredith Corporation
Chairman of the Board: William T. Kerr
President and Chief Executive Officer: Stephen M. Lacy

In Memoriam: E.T. Meredith III (1933–2003)

All of us at Meredith Consumer Marketing are dedicated to
providing you with information and ideas to enhance your home.
We welcome your comments and suggestions. Write to us at:
Meredith Consumer Marketing, 1716 Locust St.,
Des Moines, IA 50309-3023.

Better Homes and Gardens®
CHRISTMAS
FROM THE HEART®

contents

holiday in
RED & WHITE

Make the season happy and bright with projects that you make all in red and white.

Dress your tree for the holidays with **Festive Fabric Yo-Yos**, *above*, made using a variety of red and white fabrics and trims. Be sure to add some **Rickrack Candy Canes** and **Glimmering Button Ornaments** to complete your holiday red-and-white theme. For instructions, see pages 16–17. Turn the page to see the ornaments and trims that make this tree the center of attention.

Rickrack Candy Canes, *below left*, will have guests taking a second look. These clever little faux candy-cane trims are created by intertwining red and white rickrack and then stiffening the fabric with crafts glue. **Glimmering Button Ornaments**, *below right*, are simple to make using white buttons and a dusting of white glitter. For instructions, see pages 16–17.

Greet guests in a big way with a **Big Gifty Welcome**, *above*.
Large cardboard boxes are covered with a variety of red-and-white print
wrapping papers, stacked, and then tied together with an assortment of
wide ribbon. The pretty present is then topped with a large bow, greenery,
cinnamon sticks, and a merry gift tag. For instructions, see page 17.

This year make Christmas stockings in the striking color combination of red and white. A simple red and white striped print combined with a rickrack trim becomes a delightful **Candy Cane Stripe Stocking**, *above right.* Use red trims, embroidery floss, sequins, and beads to create a stunning **Embroidered Holiday Stocking**, *right.* A bright red ribbon threaded through a golden belt buckle becomes the cuff for the **Christmas Red Stocking**, *below right.* For patterns and instructions for all the stockings, see pages 17–19.

Add a bright and festive touch to holiday packages with **Personally Perfect Gift Tags**, *below*. Bits of colored ribbons, alphabet and winter-white stickers, and punched trims ensure that each tag is uniquely designed. For instructions see page 19.

Napkin trims will become conversation pieces when you make

Zipper-Roses Napkin Rings, *above,* for your holiday table. The clever

and sweet roses are made with simple zippers coiled and stitched to

resemble an elegant flower. Add a pin closure to the back of the rose so it

can be worn as jewelry after the holiday meal. Instructions are on page 20.

A simple tabletop is stunning when you choose red and white as the main colors. Red or white napkins topped with crisscrossed white-handled flatware and red-and-white polka-dot ornaments resting in tumblers make the table fun as well as festive. White kitchen canisters topped with green moss finish the look. For instructions to create this **Casual Holiday Tabletop**, *above*, see page 20.

Stitch playful white swirls and pom-poms to decorate a knitted red stocking to create a **Swirled Stocking,** *left.* The swirls are embroidered after the stocking is knitted, and the duplicate-stitch letters personalize each stocking. Instructions are on pages 20–21.

Festive Fabric Yo-Yos

Shown on pages 6–7

WHAT YOU NEED
FOR ONE ORNAMENT
Tracing paper
Pencil
Scissors
9-inch square of cotton fabric
4-inch piece of cardboard
Matching sewing thread
Buttons, lace, rickrack, or other trims
Fabric glue

WHAT YOU DO
1. Enlarge and trace circle patterns, *below*, onto tracing paper and cut out. For each ornament, cut out one large circle from cotton fabric and one small circle from cardboard.
2. To make yo-yo, fold in about ⅛ inch on edge of fabric circle to wrong side and sew by hand using medium-length basting stitches. Use two strands of sewing thread or heavy button and carpet thread to prevent thread from breaking. Lay small cardboard circle in center of wrong side of the fabric circle. Pull up thread tightly to draw the fabric up in a small center circle over the cardboard. Tie off thread to secure.
3. With fabric glue, secure scraps of laces, rickrack, and other trims to inside or outside of yo-yo. Glue buttons to center, if desired. Loop a 9-inch length of trim at top back for hanger and glue in place.

Rickrack Candy Canes

Shown on pages 5, 7, 8

WHAT YOU NEED
Red jumbo rickrack
White jumbo rickrack
Fabric stiffener; straight pins
Clear nylon thread for hangers
Plastic wrap

WHAT YOU DO
1. Weave red and white rickrack together to make a long rope. Lay twisted length flat on ironing board and steam-press flat. For each ornament, cut a length about 8 inches long and secure ends with straight pins.
2. Dip trim in fabric stiffener and work into trim. Squeeze out excess liquid, shape into candy cane shape, and lay it flat on plastic wrap to dry. When dry, cut ends straight across trim. Loop nylon thread over curve of candy cane and knot ends to make hanger.

FESTIVE FABRIC YO-YOS
Fabric
Enlarge 200%

FESTIVE FABRIC YO-YOS
Cardboard
Enlarge 200%

Glimmering Button Ornaments
Shown on pages 5, 7, 8

WHAT YOU NEED
FOR ONE ORNAMENT
Purchased matte finish white ball-style ornament
Crafts glue
10-inch piece of ¼-inch-wide white satin ribbon
Small clear white buttons
Fine white glitter
Narrow ribbon for hanging

WHAT YOU DO
1. Be sure the ornament is clean and dry. Starting at the top of the ornament, use crafts glue to adhere the ribbon all the way around the ornament. Trim off any remaining ribbon. Allow to dry.
2. Glue the buttons onto the ribbon, gluing a few at a time and allowing to dry before gluing on remaining buttons. Run a line of glue around the buttons and dust with glitter. Use your finger to make dots of thin glue on the remaining part of the ornament; dust with glitter. Allow to dry. Attach ribbon to hang.

Big Gifty Welcome
Shown on page 9

WHAT YOU NEED
3 large cardboard boxes in graduated sizes
3 large rolls of wrapping paper in desired patterns
Wide transparent tape or packaging tape

3 styles of wide ribbon in desired patterns
Double-stick tape
10-inch-long cinnamon sticks
Artificial greenery and berries
4×11-inch piece of red paper
White alphabet stickers
Paper punch
Scissors
Narrow ribbon

WHAT YOU DO
1. Wrap the boxes using the wrapping paper. *Note:* Because the boxes are so big use plenty of wide transparent tape or packaging tape to secure. Wrap the ribbon around the boxes in pieces, keeping them flat and using plenty of tape. Tape securely at the bottom of each package.
2. Stack the packages atop each other, securing with double-stick tape between boxes. Make a large bow and tape to the top box. Tuck in cinnamon sticks, sprigs of greenery, and berries.
3. To make a tag, cut a point on the narrow end of the red paper. Using white alphabet stickers spell out "Merry Christmas." Punch a hole in the end and use narrow ribbon to hang on the top of the box, taping to secure.

Candy Cane Stripe Stocking
Shown on pages 7, 10, 11

WHAT YOU NEED
Tracing paper; pencil
Scissors
Straight pins
Needle; matching thread

Clear nylon thread
1 yard *each* red and white jumbo rickrack
1 yard 1½-inch-wide gigantic decorative red rickrack
½ yard red-and-white-striped cotton fabric
½ yard white cotton lining fabric
6 mm silver beads

WHAT YOU DO
1. Enlarge and trace pattern, *page 19*, and cut out. Cut two stocking pieces each from the striped and lining fabrics. Weave red and white jumbo rickrack together to intertwine. Trim will tend to spiral or twist, so gently steam press to make it lie flat. Using clear nylon thread, sew trim around stocking front to make heel and toe lines.
2. With right sides together, stitch stocking front to back, using ¼-inch seam line to stitch around side and lower edges. With right sides together stitch ¼-inch seam line to join lining pieces together around side and lower edges, leaving an opening for turning. Clip seams and turn. Press lightly.

3. For the cuff, cut a 5½×16½-inch piece from the striped fabric and lining fabric. Stitch the short ends together for each piece. Turn to the right side. With right sides together, stitch lining to cuff along the bottom edge. Clip seam and turn to right side. Using clear nylon thread, sew red and white rickrack trim to bottom edge of cuff. Baste cuff to stocking top edge.

4. From the striped fabric, cut a 2×8-inch strip for the hanger. With right sides together, fold strip in half lengthwise and sew along long edge, using a ¼-inch seam. Turn right side out and press. Fold length in half and align top edges of hanger even with top edge of stocking at side seam, having fold extend down into stocking. Baste across top. Slip the stocking into the lining with right sides facing. Stitch around top edge. Pull the stocking through the lining opening. Stitch lining opening closed. Work the lining inside the stocking and press the top edge flat.

5. To make red rickrack poinsettias, cut rickrack into lengths of 5 to 7 complete bumps. Fold one bump together along diagonal edge and stitch along top edge using matching sewing thread. Fold another bump together and stitch down that top length, stitching points together in the center. Continue around the length to form pointed poinsettia petals. Fold cut ends to the back and stitch to back side. Sew five silver beads to center of each flower. Tack to stocking cuff by taking a few stitches underneath flowers and through cuff.

Embroidered Holiday Stocking
Shown on pages 7, 10, 11

WHAT YOU NEED
Tracing paper; pencil; scissors
Straight pins
Needle; matching thread
½ yard white woven linen fabric
½ yard white lining fabric
12-inch-long pieces of red ribbon, laces, rickrack, cording, and other assorted trims
6 mm white pearl beads
Assorted red beads
Red sequins
Red and white embroidery floss

WHAT YOU DO
1. Enlarge and trace pattern, *page 19*, and cut out. Cut two stocking pieces each from the linen and lining fabrics. Overcast edges of top linen stocking piece.

2. Lay out assorted ribbons and trims in straight horizontal rows across stocking front. Pin in place. Stitch trims in place. Make decorative stitches with embroidery floss as desired. *Note:* For stitch diagrams, *see pages 19 and 159.* Hand stitch beads in centers of sequins and along some stitching.

3. With right sides together, stitch stocking front to back, using ¼-inch seam line to stitch around side and lower edges. With right sides together, stitch ¼-inch seam line to join lining pieces around side and lower edges, leaving an opening for turning. Clip seams and turn. Press lightly.

4. From the linen fabric, cut a 2×8-inch strip for the hanger. With right sides together, fold strip in half lengthwise and sew along long edge in ¼-inch seam. Turn right side out and press. Fold length in half and align top edges of hanger even with top edge of stocking at side seam,

having fold extend down into stocking. Baste across top. Slip the stocking into the lining with right sides facing. Stitch around top edge. Pull the stocking through the lining opening. Stitch lining opening closed. Work the lining inside the stocking and press the top edge flat.

Christmas Red Stocking
Shown on pages 7, 10, 11

WHAT YOU NEED
Tracing paper
Pencil
Scissors
Straight pins
Needle; matching thread
½ yard red embroidered suede-like fabric
½ yard red lining fabric
6 mm white pearl beads
Assorted red sequins
¾ yard of 3-inch-wide red satin ribbon
1¼ yard white cording
Decorative pearl brooch

WHAT YOU DO

1. Enlarge and trace pattern, *right*, and cut out. Cut two stocking pieces each from the suede and lining fabrics. Sew sequins and pearls to stocking front. Stitch cording around the stocking front side and lower edges.

2. With right sides together, stitch stocking front to back, using ¼-inch seam line to stitch around side and lower edges. With right sides together, stitch ¼-inch seam line to join lining pieces around side and lower edges, leaving an opening for turning. Clip seams and turn. Press lightly.

3. From the suede fabric, cut a 2×8-inch strip for the hanger. With right sides together, fold strip in half lengthwise and sew along long edge in ¼-inch seam. Turn right side out and press. Fold length in half and align top edges of hanger even with top edge of stocking at side seam, having fold extend down into stocking. Baste across top. Slip the stocking into the lining with right sides facing. Stitch around top edge. Pull the stocking through the lining opening. Stitch lining opening closed. Work the lining inside the stocking and press the top edge flat.

4. Wrap wide satin ribbon around stocking at top edge. Loop ends over as if tying a knot. Tack ribbon to side edges of stocking by taking a few hand stitches with needle and thread of a matching color. Secure ribbon to side of stocking with a decorative pearl brooch.

Personally Perfect Gift Tags

Shown on page 12

WHAT YOU NEED

Scraps of white and red cardstock
Scraps of printed scrapbook paper
Scraps of red and white ribbon
Alphabet stickers
Snowflake stickers
Crafts glue
Paper punch
Scissors; decorative scissors

WHAT YOU DO

For the Joy Tag: Cut white cardstock into a 4-inch square. Use decorative scissors to scallop the top edge. Use a paper punch to punch 6 holes across the top of the paper. Thread a red ribbon through the holes. Fold over 1½ inches from the top. Spell "Joy" on the flap using alphabet stickers. Add

snowflake stickers around the letters. Punch a hole in the corner and tie a narrow ribbon for hanging.

For the Noel Tag: Cut white cardstock into a 3½-inch square. Spell "Noel" with alphabet stickers. Glue a ½×3½-inch strip of printed scrapbook paper at the bottom of the tag. Glue a scrap of white ribbon at the top of the printed paper. Punch a hole in the corner and tie a narrow ribbon for hanging.

CANDY CANE STRIPE, EMBROIDERED HOLIDAY, AND CHRISTMAS RED STOCKINGS
Enlarge 400%
Cut 2 fabric, reversing one
Cut 2 lining, reversing one
(add ¼" seam allowance)

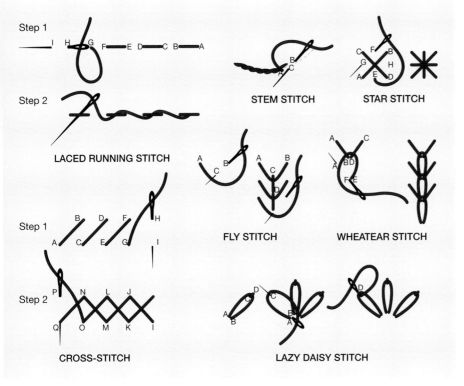

STEP 1 / STEP 2 — **LACED RUNNING STITCH**

STEM STITCH

STAR STITCH

FLY STITCH

WHEATEAR STITCH

STEP 1 / STEP 2 — **CROSS-STITCH**

LAZY DAISY STITCH

holiday in red & white

For the Red Snowflake Card: Cut red cardstock into a 3½×5-inch rectangle. Fold in half. Place a large snowflake sticker on the front in the center. Cut two pieces of ribbon each 5½ inches long and glue to the sides of the card. Cut a 3×4¼-inch piece of white cardstock. Glue to the inside front of the card.

For the White Snowflake Card: Cut white cardstock into a 4½-inch square. Fold down top 1½ inches and trim with decorative scissors. Glue a piece of red ribbon under the flap. Decorate with white snowflake stickers.

For the Ribbon Tag: Cut a 2½-inch-wide ribbon 4 inches long. Notch the bottom of the ribbon and point the top of the ribbon. Add alphabet stickers to spell out the monogram. Glue a scrap of ribbon to the top for hanging. Add a sticker at the top.

Zipper-Roses Napkin Rings
Shown on page 13

WHAT YOU NEED
One 22–24-inch metal-tooth zipper or plastic-tooth zipper
Needle
Matching sewing thread
¼-inch-wide ribbon
Fabric glue (optional)

WHAT YOU DO
1. Open and separate zipper in two pieces (one complete zipper can make two flowers). Start at one end and roll zipper into a tight coil. Hand-sew coil together at the bottom by taking a few hand stitches through zipper tape. Continue stitching a running stitch at the bottom of the zipper tape to gather the tape to make a flower petal. Tack in place by sewing through tape at the bottom edge of tape.
2. Continue forming petals with a running stitch at the bottom of the tape, tacking in place around the center coil until the zipper end is reached. Sew or glue ribbon to back of finished rose zipper. Tie around napkin.

Casual Holiday Tabletop
Shown on page 14

The tabletop is created using red and white place mats, plates, and napkins, mixing and matching each place setting as desired. The table is first covered with fringed woven off-white fabric. The settings are placed and white handled flatware is crisscrossed over the napkin with fresh greenery tucked underneath. Purchased red-and-white polka-dot ornaments rest on tall tumblers. The centerpiece is created by filling white canisters with newspaper and then topping with green moss. Name tags are hand written using a red marker on white cardstock, then tucked under the polka-dot ornaments.

Swirled Stocking
Shown on page 15

SKILL LEVEL: Intermediate
FINISHED MEASUREMENTS:
Finished length to heel is approx. 17 inches.

WHAT YOU NEED
80% acrylic/20% wool bulky-weight yarn: one 5 oz/153 yard skein each of red (MC) and cream (CC) (We used Lion Brand Wool-Ease, Art. 630 in Red #112 and Fisherman #099.)
Size 10½ double-pointed needles or size needed to obtain gauge
Stitch marker; blunt-end yarn needle
Pom-pom maker

GAUGE: 12 sts and 16 rnds = 4 inches In St st. TAKE TIME TO CHECK YOUR GAUGE.

WHAT YOU DO
KNIT THE STOCKING
Note: For abbreviations, see *page 159.*

Stocking Top
Beg at top with MC, cast on 64 sts. Keeping sts untwisted, arrange onto 3 dpns; place marker for beg, join. K42, bind off 22 sts for hanging loop. Rearrange the 42 sts onto 3 needles and 3 rnds. Change to CC and k 11 rnds. Change to MC and k 43 rnds.

Heel
Setup for heel: Place first and last 11 sts onto one dpn, then place rem 20 sts onto a second dpn for holder. Working back and forth in St st on the 22 sts and using CC, beg with a p row and work 11 rows total; end with a p row.
Heel turn Row 1: Slip 1-k, k14, ssk, k; turn.
Row 2: Slip 1-p, p9, p2tog; turn.
Row 3: Slip 1-k, k9, ssk; turn.
Rep last 2 rows until 11 sts rem, ending with a RS row. In following instructions, this needle will be called #1. Break the yarn.

Gusset
With RS facing, using MC and needle #1, pick up and k 7 sts evenly spaced along side of heel. With needle #2, k20 (instep sts). With needle #3, pick up and k 7 sts evenly spaced along side of heel, k6 from needle #1—13 sts.
Rnd 1: K9, ssk, k1 (#1). *Note:* This is the first time the first 5 sts will be worked

with MC, and there will be 12 sts on this needle before working the rnd. K20 (#2); k1, k2tog, k10 (#3)–43 sts.

Rnd 2: K around.
Rnd 3: K8, ssk, k1; k20; k1; k2tog, k9–41 sts.
Rnd 4: K around.
Rnd 5: K7, ssk, k1; k20; k1, k2tog, k8–39 sts.

Work even on 39 sts until the piece measures 5 inches from pick-up rnd.

Toe
Rnd 1: With MC, k6, ssk, k1 (#1); k1, k2tog, k14, ssk, k1 (#2); k1, k2tog, k7 (#3)–35 sts.
Rnd 2: Knit.
Rnd 3: With MC, k5, ssk, k1; k1, k2tog, k12, ssk, k1; k1, k2tog, k6–31 sts. Change to CC for remainder of stocking.
Rnd 4: Knit.
Rnd 5: With CC, k4, ssk, k1; k1, k2tog, k10, ssk, k1; k1, k2tog, k5–27 sts.
Rnd 6: K3, ssk, k1; k1, k2tog, k8, ssk, k1; k1, k2tog, k4–23 sts.
Rnd 7: K2, ssk, k1; k1, k2tog, k6, ssk, k1; k1, k2tog, k3–19 sts.
Rnd 8: K1, ssk, k1; k1, k2tog, k4, ssk, k1; k1, k2tog, k2–15 sts.
Rnd 9: Ssk, k1; k1, k2tog, k2, ssk, k1; k1, k2tog, k1–11 sts.

To complete, k2 on #1; k1, k2 tog, ssk, k1 on #2; k3 on #3, then with same needle, k2tog from #1–8 sts with 4 on each of two needles. Cut the yarn, leaving a 10-inch tail.

JOIN THE TOE
To graft stockinette stitches, hold wrong sides together with the needles pointed to the right. Thread the yarn tail onto a yarn needle. *Insert the yarn needle knitwise through the first stitch on the front needle and let the stitch drop from the needle. See diagram, *below right.*

Insert the yarn needle into the second stitch on the front needle purlwise and pull the yarn through, leaving the stitch on the needle.

Insert the yarn needle into the first stitch on the back needle purlwise and let it drop from the needle. Insert the yarn needle knitwise through the second stitch on the back needle and pull the yarn through, leaving the stitch on the needle. Repeat from * across until all stitches have been joined. Adjust the tension as necessary. Weave in loose ends.

FINISH THE STOCKING
Fold the top MC edge in half and sew it in place along the wrong side, leaving the hanging loop free.

Embroider the swirl designs. Separate one ply of CC from a 24-inch strand. Thread it into a yarn needle and chain-stitch the swirled design. For chain-stitch directions, see *below*.

Using MC, duplicate-stitch letters onto the cuff area of the stocking, referring to the alphabet chart, *below*. For duplicate-stitch directions, see *left*. To finish, trim the yarn and weave in the ends on backside.

Using the pom-pom maker and CC, make 8 pom-poms the desired size. Sew them in place about 1 inch apart along the top edge.

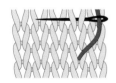  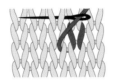

DUPLICATE STITCH

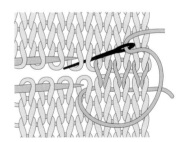

GRAFTING STOCKINETTE STITCHES

CHAIN STITCH

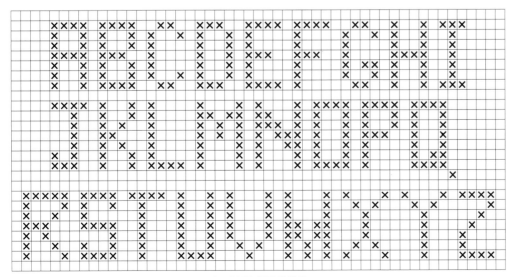

SWIRLED STOCKING
Alphabet Chart

cookies
by the dozen

Give this year's holiday cookie packages a new spin with these beauties. The tradition of baking and sharing cookies is something family and friends will always remember.

Get ready for the best sampler yet—drops, slices, cutouts, and impressions—all simply embellished to stand out. Recipes begin on page 31.

Like the season's first snowfall, snowflake cookies set the mood adrift for a white Christmas. Using an array of cutters and festive candies, you're sure to unleash a flurry of designs for these **Stained-Glass Snowflakes**. Recipe is on page 31. See information for ordering snowflake cutters on page 159.

Intriguing flavor combinations create the most incredible cookies. Chopped-up candy canes bring a burst of freshness to **Triple-Chocolate Cookies**, *above left.* Chunks of crystallized ginger add a nice spicy bite to **Honey-Ginger Bites**, *below left.*

Recipes are on page 32.

Anything chocolate is always a hit. Here, chocolate melds with warm spices in **Chunky Chocolate and Chai Biscotti**, *above*, and creates ooey-gooey goodness in **Deluxe Caramel-Nut Brownies**, *right*. Recipes are on pages 32–33.

Take a bite out of winter's chill by mixing up a batch of buttery
Brown Sugar Shortbreads, *above left,* or awaken your senses by
adding fragrant, warm ingredients to **Spicy Ginger Crinkles**,
above right. Recipes are on pages 33–34.

Create baked works of art using colorful embellishments and simple decorating techniques. The **Classic Spritz Cookies**, *opposite*, **Gingerbread Family**, *above*, and **Christmas Sandies**, *left,* taste as terrific as they look. Recipes are on pages 34–35. See information for ordering cookie cutters on page 159.

A handful of nuts adds pleasing crunch and depth of flavor to bars and cookies. **Cherry-Walnut Blondies,** *above,* and **Nutmeg-Pumpkin Drops,** *right,* demonstrate this concept deliciously. Recipes are on page 35.

Cherry-Nut Pinwheels
Shown on page 23

WHAT YOU NEED
- ¾ cup butter, softened
- 1 cup granulated sugar
- ½ teaspoon baking powder
- ¼ teaspoon salt
- 1 egg
- 1 teaspoon vanilla
- 1 teaspoon cherry extract or 2 teaspoons Kirsch
- 2 cups all-purpose flour
  Red paste food coloring
- ¼ cup ground almonds
  Coarse sanding sugar (optional)

WHAT YOU DO
1. In a large bowl beat butter with an electric mixer on medium to high for 30 seconds. Add granulated sugar, baking powder, and salt. Beat until combined, scraping bowl occasionally. Beat in egg, vanilla, and cherry extract or Kirsch until combined. Beat in as much of the flour as you can with the mixer. Using a wooden spoon, stir in any remaining flour.
2. Divide dough in half. Tint one dough portion with red food coloring. Stir or knead the ground almonds into the remaining dough portion. Cover and chill dough portions about 1 hour or until firm.
3. On a lightly floured pastry cloth or tea towel, roll almond dough portion into a 12×8-inch rectangle. On a piece of waxed paper, roll red dough portion into a 12×8-inch rectangle. Invert red dough rectangle over almond dough rectangle; peel off waxed paper. Roll up into a spiral,

starting from a long side. Pinch to seal. Wrap in plastic wrap or waxed paper. Chill for 1 to 2 hours or until firm. If desired, roll dough in sanding sugar.
4. Preheat oven to 375°F. Remove dough log from the refrigerator. Unwrap. If necessary, reshape slightly. Cut roll into ¼-inch-thick slices. Arrange slices about 2 inches apart on ungreased cookie sheet. If desired, sprinkle with more coarse sugar. Bake for 8 to 10 minutes or until tops are set. Transfer cookies to a wire rack; let cool. Makes about 48 cookies.
To Store: Layer cookies between waxed paper in an airtight container; cover. Store at room temperature up to 3 days or freeze up to 3 months.
To Make Ahead: Prepare log as directed. Place log in an airtight container; cover. Refrigerate up to 3 days or freeze up to 3 months. Thaw overnight in refrigerator before slicing.

Stained-Glass Snowflakes
Shown on page 24

WHAT YOU NEED
- ½ cup butter, softened
- ½ cup sugar
- ¼ teaspoon salt
- 1 egg
- 1½ teaspoons light-color corn syrup
- 1 teaspoon finely shredded lemon peel
- 1 teaspoon lemon extract
- 1¾ cups all-purpose flour
- 3 ounces assorted fruit-flavor hard candy
  Powdered Sugar Icing

WHAT YOU DO
1. Preheat oven to 375°F. In a large mixing bowl beat butter on medium to high for 30 seconds. Add sugar and salt. Beat until combined, scraping bowl occasionally. Beat in egg, corn syrup, lemon peel, and lemon extract until combined. Beat in as much of the flour as you can. Stir in any remaining flour. Divide dough in half. If necessary, cover and chill dough in the refrigerator about 30 minutes or until easy to handle.
2. On a lightly floured surface, roll half the dough at a time to ⅛-inch thickness. Using floured snowflake cookie cutters, cut dough. Place 1 inch apart on a foil-lined cookie sheet. Cut small shapes out of cookie centers. Reroll trimmings.
3. Separate hard candies by color. Place each color in a small, heavy resealable plastic bag; seal bag. Finely crush candy. Spoon some of the crushed candy into each center cutout, completely filling to the same thickness as cookies.
4. Bake for 7 to 8 minutes or until bottoms are lightly browned. Transfer cookie sheet to a wire rack; let cookies cool on foil. Peel foil from backs of cookies. Decorate with Powdered Sugar Icing. Makes 2 to 3 dozen cookies.
Powdered Sugar Icing: Combine 2 cups powdered sugar and 2 to 3 teaspoons milk to make icing of piping consistency.
To Store: Layer unfrosted cookies between waxed paper in an airtight container; cover. Store at room temperature up to 3 days or freeze up to 3 months. Pipe with icing before serving.

cookies by the dozen

Triple-Chocolate Cookies

Shown on page 25

WHAT YOU NEED

- 7 ounces bittersweet chocolate, chopped
- 5 ounces unsweetened chocolate, chopped
- ½ cup butter
- ⅓ cup all-purpose flour
- ¼ teaspoon baking powder
- ¼ teaspoon salt
- 1 cup granulated sugar
- ¾ cup packed brown sugar
- 4 eggs
- ¼ cup finely chopped pecans, toasted*
- 1 cup semisweet chocolate pieces
- 4 teaspoons shortening
  Crushed peppermint candy (optional)

WHAT YOU DO

1. In a 2-quart saucepan combine chocolates and butter. Heat and stir on low heat until smooth. Remove from heat. Let cool for 10 minutes. In a small bowl stir together flour, baking powder, and salt; set aside.

2. In a large mixing bowl combine sugars and eggs. Beat with an electric mixer on medium to high for 2 to 3 minutes or until color lightens slightly. Beat in melted chocolate mixture. Add flour mixture to chocolate mixture; heat until combined. Stir in pecans. Cover surface of cookie dough with plastic wrap. Let stand for 20 minutes (dough will thicken as it stands).

3. Preheat oven to 350°F. Line cookie sheets with parchment paper or foil. Drop dough by rounded teaspoons 2 inches apart on prepared cookie sheets. Bake about 9 minutes or just until tops are set.

Cool on cookie sheet for 1 minute. Transfer to wire racks and let cool.

4. For chocolate drizzle, in a small saucepan combine semisweet chocolate pieces and shortening. Cook and stir on low heat until chocolate melts and is smooth. Remove from heat.

5. Place cooled cookies on a cookie sheet lined with parchment or waxed paper. Drizzle melted chocolate over tops of cookies. If desired, sprinkle tops of cookies with crushed peppermint candy. Place the entire cookie sheet in the freezer for 4 to 5 minutes or until chocolate is firm. Remove from freezer. Makes about 60 cookies.

To Store: Place cookies in single layer in an airtight container; cover. Store at room temperature up to 3 days.

*Test Kitchen Tip: To toast pecans, spread them in a shallow pan. Bake them in a 350°F oven for 5 to 10 minutes, stirring often so they don't burn.

Honey-Ginger Bites

Shown on page 25

WHAT YOU NEED

- ⅓ cup honey
- ¼ cup butter
- 2 cups all-purpose flour
- ¼ cup granulated sugar
- 3 tablespoons finely chopped crystallized ginger
- ½ teaspoon baking soda
- ¼ teaspoon white pepper (optional)
- 1 egg, lightly beaten
  Powdered sugar

WHAT YOU DO

1. In a small saucepan combine honey and butter. Cook and stir on low heat

until butter melts. Remove from heat. Pour mixture into a large bowl and cool to room temperature.

2. In a medium bowl stir together the flour, granulated sugar, ginger, baking soda, and, if desired, pepper. Set aside.

3. Stir egg into cooled honey mixture. Gradually stir in flour mixture; knead in the last of the flour mixture by hand, if necessary. Cover and chill about 1 hour or until dough is easy to handle.

4. Preheat oven to 350°F. Divide dough into 12 portions.* On a lightly floured surface, roll each dough portion into a 10-inch-long rope. Cut each rope into ½-inch pieces. Place the dough pieces about ½ inch apart in an ungreased shallow baking pan.

5. Bake for 6 to 8 minutes or until tops are very lightly browned. Transfer cookies to paper towels to cool. Roll in powdered sugar. Makes about 240 small cookies.

To Store: Layer cookies between sheets of waxed paper in an airtight container; cover. Store at room temperature up to 3 days or freeze up to 3 months.

*Test Kitchen Tip: To divide dough into 12 equal portions, shape dough into a 12-inch log; cut log into 1-inch pieces.

Chunky Chocolate and Chai Biscotti

Shown on page 26

WHAT YOU NEED

- 2¾ cups all-purpose flour
- ½ cup sugar
- ¼ cup instant chai latte mix
- 1½ teaspoons baking powder
- 1 teaspoon instant espresso coffee powder or instant coffee crystals
- ¼ teaspoon salt
- 3 eggs

6 tablespoons butter, melted
1 teaspoon vanilla
1 cup chopped coffee-flavor chocolate bar (about 5¼ ounces)
2 ounces white baking chocolate
1 tablespoon semisweet chocolate chips

WHAT YOU DO

1. Preheat oven to 325°F. Lightly grease a large cookie sheet; set aside. In a large bowl stir together flour, sugar, latte mix, baking powder, espresso powder, and salt. In a medium bowl whisk together eggs, butter, and vanilla. Add egg mixture to flour mixture and stir until well combined. Stir in chopped chocolate.
2. Divide dough in half. Shape each portion into a 12-inch log about 1½ inches in diameter. Place logs 4 inches apart on prepared cookie sheet.
3. Bake for 25 to 30 minutes or until tops are lightly browned and cracked. Cool on cookie sheet on a wire rack for 15 minutes.
4. Transfer baked logs to a cutting board. Using a serrated knife, cut each log diagonally into ½-inch-thick slices. Place slices, flat sides down, on ungreased cookie sheets. Bake for 8 minutes. Turn slices over; bake 8 to 10 minutes more or until crisp and lightly browned. Transfer to wire racks; let cool.
5. For chocolate icing, in a small saucepan heat white baking chocolate and chocolate chips on low heat until melted. Partially dip biscotti into melted chocolate. Cool on wax paper-lined cookie sheet until chocolate sets up. Makes about 30 cookies.

To Store: Store undecorated cookies in airtight containers at room temperature up to 2 days or in the freezer up to 3 months. Thaw and ice with chocolate.

Deluxe Caramel-Nut Brownies
Shown on page 26

WHAT YOU NEED
1 cup butter, softened
2 cups packed brown sugar
6 ounces dark or bittersweet chocolate baking bar, chopped and melted
4 eggs
2 teaspoons vanilla
1 cup all-purpose flour

1 12-ounce package semisweet chocolate pieces
1 cup chopped pecans, toasted*
24 vanilla caramels, unwrapped, or 1 cup caramel bits
2 tablespoons milk

WHAT YOU DO
1. Preheat oven to 350°F. Line a 13×9×2-inch baking pan with heavy foil, extending foil over the pan edges. Lightly grease foil. Set pan aside. In a mixing bowl beat butter on medium to high for 30 seconds. Add brown sugar; beat until fluffy. Add melted chocolate, beating until blended. Beat in eggs and vanilla. Beat in flour until well combined. Stir in chocolate pieces and pecans.
2. Spread half the brownie batter in prepared pan. Bake for 15 minutes. Meanwhile, in a heavy medium saucepan cook and stir unwrapped caramels and milk on medium-low heat until melted and smooth; drizzle over partially baked brownies. Spoon remaining brownie batter over caramel layer; spread evenly.
3. Bake for 25 to 30 minutes more or until edges are set and top appears dry. Cool in pan on a wire rack. Using the edges of the foil, lift uncut brownies out of pan. Use a hot knife to cut into bars. Makes 32 bars.

To Store: Layer bars between sheets of waxed paper in an airtight container; cover. Store at room temperature up to 3 days or freeze up to 3 months.
*Test Kitchen Tip: To toast pecans, spread them in a shallow pan. Bake them in a 350°F oven for 5 to 10 minutes, stirring often so they don't burn.

Brown Sugar Shortbreads
Shown on page 27

WHAT YOU NEED
1 cup butter, softened
½ cup packed brown sugar
½ teaspoon apple pie spice or pumpkin pie spice
⅛ teaspoon salt
2¼ cups all-purpose flour
Nonstick cooking spray
Granulated sugar

WHAT YOU DO
1. Preheat oven to 350°F. Line a cookie sheet with parchment paper; set aside. In a large bowl beat butter on medium to high for 30 seconds. Add brown sugar, apple pie spice, and salt. Beat until combined, scraping bowl occasionally. Beat in as much of the flour as you can. Stir in any remaining flour.
2. Shape dough into 1-inch balls. Place balls 2 inches apart on prepared cookie sheet. Coat bottom of a glass or cookie stamp with cooking spray and dip in granulated sugar. Flatten each cookie with the glass or stamp, imprinting the pattern.
3. Bake for 12 to 15 minutes or until lightly browned. Transfer cookies to a wire rack; cool. Makes about 36 cookies.
To Store: Layer cookies between sheets of waxed paper in an airtight container; cover. Store at room temperature up to 3 days or freeze up to 3 months.

Spicy Ginger Crinkles
Shown on page 27

WHAT YOU NEED
- ¾ cup butter, softened
- 1 cup packed brown sugar
- 2 teaspoons baking soda
- 2 teaspoons ground ginger
- 1 teaspoon ground cinnamon
- ¾ teaspoon salt
- ¼ teaspoon ground cloves
- ¼ teaspoon ground allspice
- 1 egg
- ¼ cup full-flavor molasses
- 1 teaspoon vanilla
- 2¼ cups all-purpose flour
- 2 tablespoons finely chopped crystallized ginger
  Coarse sanding sugar

WHAT YOU DO
1. Preheat oven to 350°F. In a mixing bowl beat butter on medium for 30 seconds. Add brown sugar, baking soda, ground ginger, cinnamon, salt, cloves, and allspice. Beat until combined, scraping bowl occasionally. Beat in egg, molasses, and vanilla until smooth. Beat in as much flour as you can. Stir in remaining flour and crystallized ginger. If necessary, cover and chill for 1 to 2 hours or until dough is easy to handle.
2. Place coarse sanding sugar in a small bowl. Shape dough into 1¼-inch balls; roll balls in sanding sugar to coat. Place balls 2 inches apart on ungreased cookie sheet.
3. Bake about 10 minutes or until tops are crackled and edges are firm. Transfer cookies to a wire rack; let cool. Makes about 42 cookies.
To Store: Layer cookies between waxed paper in an airtight container; cover. Store at room temperature up to 3 days or freeze up to 3 months.

Classic Spritz Cookies
Shown on page 28

WHAT YOU NEED
- 1½ cups butter, softened
- 1 cup packed brown sugar
- 1 teaspoon baking powder
- 1 egg
- 1 teaspoon vanilla
- ½ teaspoon almond extract
- 3½ cups all-purpose flour
  Coarse sugar, nonpareils, edible glitter, and/or silver dragées
  Powdered Sugar Icing

WHAT YOU DO
1. Preheat oven to 375°F. In a large mixing bowl beat butter on medium to high for 30 seconds. Add brown sugar and baking powder. Beat until combined, scraping bowl occasionally. Beat in egg, vanilla, and almond extract until combined. Beat in as much flour as you can. Stir in any remaining flour.
2. Force unchilled dough through a cookie press fitted with desired disk onto an ungreased cookie sheet. If desired, sprinkle cookies with sugars or candy decorations. Bake for 7 to 9 minutes or until edges are lightly browned. Transfer to a wire rack; let cool.
3. Brush tops of plain cookies with Powdered Sugar Icing and, while still wet, sprinkle with sugars or candy decorations. Arrange on waxed paper and let stand until icing is dry. Makes about 7 dozen cookies.
Powdered Sugar Icing: Combine 2 cups powdered sugar and enough milk (2 to 3 tablespoons) to make a thin icing.
To Store: Layer cookies between sheets of waxed paper in an airtight container; cover. Store at room temperature up to 3 days or freeze up to 3 months.

Gingerbread Family
Shown on page 29

WHAT YOU NEED
- ½ cup shortening
- ½ cup granulated sugar
- 1 teaspoon baking powder
- 1 teaspoon ground ginger
- ½ teaspoon baking soda
- ½ teaspoon ground cinnamon
- ½ teaspoon ground cloves
- ½ cup molasses
- 1 egg
- 1 tablespoon vinegar
- 2½ cups all-purpose flour
  Powdered Sugar Icing
  Red food coloring
  Decorative candies

WHAT YOU DO
1. In a large mixing bowl beat shortening for 30 seconds. Add sugar, baking powder, ginger, baking soda, cinnamon, and cloves. Beat until combined, scraping sides of bowl frequently. Beat in molasses, egg, and vinegar. Beat in as much of the flour as you can. Stir in any remaining flour. Divide dough in half. Cover and chill for 3 hours or until easy to handle.
2. Preheat oven to 375°F. Grease cookie sheets; set aside. On a lightly floured surface, roll half the dough to ⅛-inch thickness. Using well-floured cutters, cut dough. Place shapes 1 inch apart on prepared cookie sheets. Bake for 5 to 6 minutes or until edges are lightly browned. Cool on cookie sheets for 1 minute. Transfer to wire racks and let cool. Repeat with remaining dough. Makes about thirty-four 5-inch cookies. Pipe designs with powdered sugar icing on cookies and add candies.
To Store: Layer undecorated cookies between waxed paper in an airtight

container; cover. Store at room temperature up to 3 days or freeze up to 3 months. Decorate before serving.
Powdered Sugar Icing: Combine 2 cups powdered sugar and enough milk (1 to 2 tablespoons) for piping consistency. Tint some icing with red food coloring.

Christmas Sandies
Shown on page 29

WHAT YOU NEED
- 1 cup butter, softened
- ½ cup powdered sugar
- 1 teaspoon vanilla
- 2 cups all-purpose flour
- 1 cup finely chopped dried cranberries
- 2 teaspoons grated lemon peel
  White, red, and green nonpareils, or pearl sugar

WHAT YOU DO
1. Preheat oven to 350°F. Line cookie sheets with parchment paper; set aside. Beat butter with an electric mixer on medium to high for 30 seconds. Add powdered sugar. Beat until combined, scraping bowl. Beat in vanilla. Beat in as much of the flour as you can with the mixer. Stir in cranberries, lemon peel, and any remaining flour (use your hands to work in flour if mixture seems crumbly).
2. Shape mixture into 1-inch balls. Roll balls in nonpareils or pearl sugar. Arrange balls 1 inch apart on prepared cookie sheets.
3. Bake for 15 minutes or until bottoms of cookies are light brown. Transfer to wire racks; let cool. Makes 36 cookies.
To Store: Layer cookies between sheets of waxed paper in an airtight container; cover. Store at room temperature up to 3 days or freeze up to 3 months.

Cherry-Walnut Blondies
Shown on page 30

WHAT YOU NEED
- ⅔ cup butter, softened
- 2 cups packed brown sugar
- 2 eggs
- 1 tablespoon cherry brandy or cherry juice (optional)
- 1½ teaspoons baking powder
- 2 teaspoons vanilla
- ¼ teaspoon salt
- 2¼ cups all-purpose flour
- 1 cup chopped walnuts, toasted*
- ¾ cup chopped white or dark sweet chocolate
- ½ cup coarsely chopped candied cherries

WHAT YOU DO
1. Preheat oven to 350°F. Lightly grease a 13×9-inch baking pan.
2. In large mixing bowl beat butter on medium to high 30 seconds. Add brown sugar; beat until well combined. Beat in eggs, brandy, baking powder, vanilla, and salt. Add flour; beat just until blended. Stir in nuts, chocolate, and cherries. Spread in prepared pan.
3. Bake 30 minutes or until golden. Cool completely in pan on wire rack. Cut in bars. Makes 24 bars.
To Store: Layer bars between sheets of waxed paper in an airtight container; cover. Store at room temperature up to 3 days or freeze up to 3 months.
*Test Kitchen Tip: To toast walnuts, spread them in a shallow pan. Bake in a 350°F oven 5 to 10 minutes, stirring the nuts often so they don't burn.

Nutmeg-Pumpkin Drops
Shown on page 30

WHAT YOU NEED
- 1 cup butter, softened
- 1 cup packed brown sugar
- 2 teaspoons freshly grated nutmeg or 1 teaspoon ground nutmeg
- 1 teaspoon baking soda
- 1 cup canned pumpkin
- 1 egg
- 2 teaspoons vanilla
- 2 cups all-purpose flour
- 2 cups white baking pieces (12 ounces)
  Pecan halves (optional)

WHAT YOU DO
1. Preheat oven to 350°F. In a large bowl beat butter with an electric mixer on medium to high for 30 seconds. Add brown sugar, nutmeg, and baking soda. Beat until combined, scraping bowl occasionally. Beat in pumpkin, egg, and vanilla until combined. Beat in as much of the flour as you can with the mixer. Using a wooden spoon, stir in any remaining flour. Stir in white baking pieces.
2. Drop dough by rounded teaspoons 2 inches apart onto an ungreased cookie sheet. If desired, press a pecan half gently onto each cookie. Bake for 11 to 14 minutes or until edges are firm. Cool on cookie sheet for 2 minutes. Transfer cookies to a wire rack; let cool. Makes about 60 cookies.
To Store: Layer cookies between sheets of waxed paper in an airtight container; cover. Store at room temperature up to 3 days or freeze up to 3 months.

Use your sewing skills and creative talents to make treasured accessories to display all through the house.

stitch IT UP!

Combine scraps of pretty green wool and tiny seed beads to make a **Christmas Holly Pin**, *above*, that is fun to wear for the holidays or to give as a special gift. Reminiscent of vintage penny rugs, this stunning **Felt Penny Pillow**, *left*, can be made using scraps of felt in any colors you wish. The little circles or penny-shape pieces of felt are stitched to a black background and then embellished with blanket stitches. For patterns and instructions, see pages 46–47.

Oh, you can catch this little gingerbread man and stitch up him up just in time for Christmas. The **Gingerbread Man Quilted Table Runner**, *above*, is pieced using vintage-color Christmas fabrics and the binding is candy-cane stripe fabric. Each little gingerbread man poses amid embroidered words to tell the story. Instructions are on pages 47–49.

Mom's Festive Flounced Apron, *opposite*, created using a pretty polka dot fabric has a large front pocket. Little Cook Apron, *above left*, is made for a preteen chef. It starts as a terry cloth dish towel and then is trimmed with white ribbon. Toddler's Apron, *above right*, is made for the youngest cook of all. Similar to Mom's, this little apron sports two bright red pockets. Instructions and patterns are on pages 50–52.

Sweet little gingerbread men hold hands or stand together to form **Felt Gingerbread Trims**, *left* and *above*. Choose felt in the tones that you like, then embellish them with clever stitches. Instructions are on pages 53–54.

Piece scraps of red and white fabric together to make **Pretty Patchwork Pincushions**, *below*. Choose your favorite quilt patterns to make each little block, or use the ones shown here. For patterns and instructions see pages 54–55.

Enjoy the beauty of wildlife this holiday with **Winter Woolen Birds**, *above*, that you can make and perch wherever you like. The beautiful birds, made using red or gold felt, have wings embellished with embroidery stitches.

So subtle in color yet so lovely, this toile fabric is perfect for a **Country Classic Stocking**, *opposite*. The stocking is faced with interfacing and then quilted following the design on the fabric. A pleated cuff and fabric gift tag finish this elegant piece. Instructions and patterns are on pages 56–57.

Felt Penny Pillow
Shown on page 36

WHAT YOU NEED

Tracing paper; pencil

18×18-inch piece of black felt for
     background

9×12-inch piece of felt in each of the
     following colors: pink, orange, red,
     burgundy, aqua, turquoise, purple,
     gold, yellow, and yellow gold

Two 9×12-inch pieces of olive green felt
     for leaves

Matching embroidery floss

Poly-fil fiberfill

2 yards of gold sew-in piping cord

18×18-inch piece of calico for back

18×18-inch piece of interfacing

 #5 red pearl cotton

15×15-inch pillow form

WHAT YOU DO

1. Measure and mark a 15×15-inch black
square of felt. Trace full-size patterns,
above, onto tracing paper and cut out.

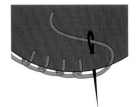

BLANKET STITCH

**SINGLE FLOWER
PLACEMENT DIAGRAM**

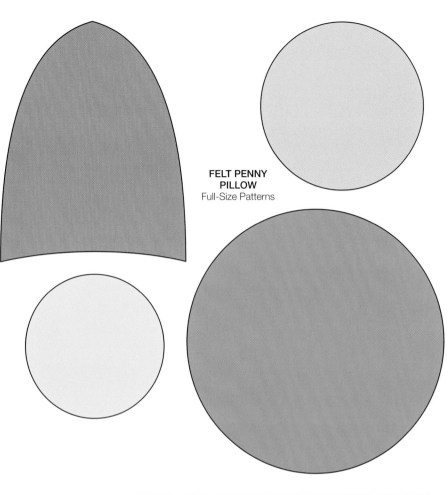

**FELT PENNY
PILLOW**
Full-Size Patterns

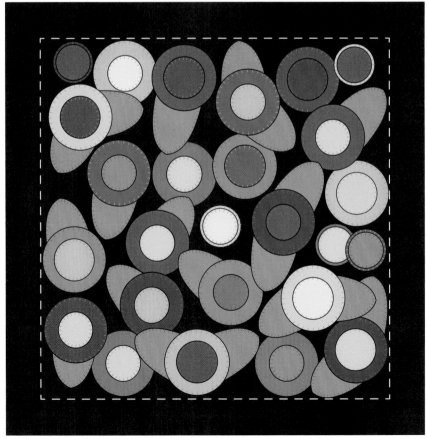

FELT PENNY PILLOW PLACEMENT DIAGRAM

Use patterns to cut various sizes of circles from felt colors as desired. Cut 20 green felt leaves.

2. Using the placement diagram, *opposite*, as a guide, pin several large circles to the black background. Blanket-stitch around each circle with three plies of matching floss. See diagram, *opposite*. Tuck leaves under circles before completing stitches. Overlap circles and leaves as necessary to make design fit. Trim short side of leaf as necessary to make various sizes.

3. Layer a contrasting small or medium circle onto the large circles and blanket-stitch around the edges. Before completing blanket stitches around the top circles, stuff with a pinch of Poly-fil. Fill in open spaces with medium and small circles.

4. Trim the pillow to ½ inch past the 15×15-inch mark. Stitch piping on marked edge. Interface calico for back and cut to same size as front. Stitch pillow front to back, right sides facing, leaving an opening for turning. Turn to right side. Insert pillow form. Stitch opening closed. To add cording, whipstitch every ¼ inch to edges using two plies of red pearl cotton.

Christmas Holly Pin
Shown on page 37

WHAT YOU NEED
Tracing paper
Pencil
Scraps of green wool
Small amount Poly-fil fiberfill
11/0 green glass seed beads
⅜-inch red beads
Matching threads
Small beading needle
1½-inch pin back

WHAT YOU DO
1. Trace pattern, *below*, onto tracing paper and cut out. For each leaf, put two layers of wool together and cut around leaf pattern. Place right sides together and stitch around leaf, using ¼-inch seam allowance and leaving an opening to turn. Trim seam; clip across points and around curves. Turn leaf shapes right sides out, pushing out at points to define shape. Stuff shapes with small amounts of Poly-fil, working stuffing into points of leaves. Using matching thread, sew openings closed.

2. Using a double thread, bring needle up at center end of leaf and thread a length of green seed beads onto the thread to make center vein line. Pull beaded length tight and insert needle into stuffed shape. Bring needle up next to beaded length to couch over beads to hold in place. Continue to make shorter vein lines in this manner, stringing beads on a length of double thread and couching lines on. Sew two holly leaves together using matching thread to stitch securing stitches on the back sides. Sew large red beads through leaf shapes. On back side, sew pin back in place.

Gingerbread Man Quilted Table Runner
Shown on pages 38–39

WHAT YOU NEED
Tracing paper; pencil
Fat quarter (18×22) or ¼ yard brown cotton fabric
Assorted ivory colored cotton fabric (to make 112 two-inch squares)
⅓ yard print cotton fabric for outside border
¼ yard red striped cotton fabric for binding
19×32-inch piece thin cotton batting
19×32-inch piece cotton fabric for backing
Ten ⅛-inch black buttons for eyes
Fourteen ¼ inch yellow buttons
16 inches red baby rickrack
20 inches white baby rickrack
2⅛ yards red medium rickrack
Embroidery floss in black, red, tan, and green
Matching sewing threads
Water soluble marking pen

WHAT YOU DO
1. Trace patterns, *pages 48–49*, and set aside. Piece together 2-inch ivory squares to make background 7 squares by 16 squares, to finish to 11×24½-inch size.

2. Cut out gingerbread man shapes from brown fabric. Appliqué gingerbread shapes on background piece. Stitch lines on arms and head with a satin machine stitch. Cut small pieces of red and white rickrack and stitch in place to embellish gingerbread shapes.

3. Using two strands of embroidery floss, stem stitch to outline details. Stitch eyebrow lines with black floss, nose with tan floss, and mouths with red floss. *Note:* For embroidery stitch diagrams and instructions see *page 159*. Using matching sewing threads, sew black buttons on shapes for eyes and yellow buttons onto fronts.

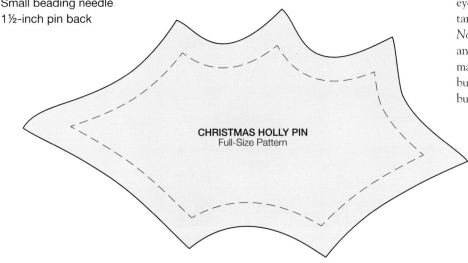

CHRISTMAS HOLLY PIN
Full-Size Pattern

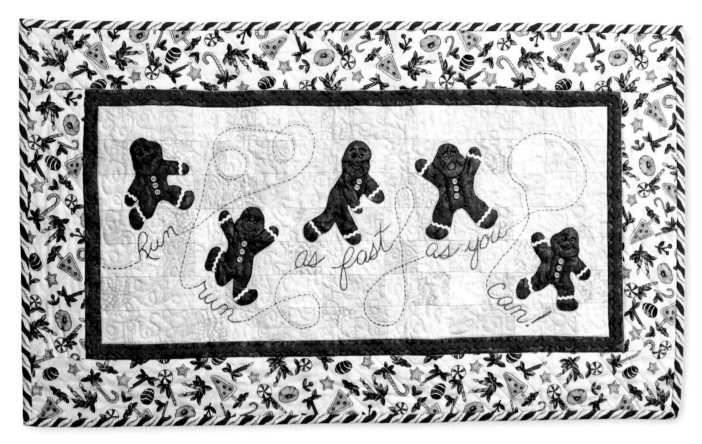

4. Mark green lines and words with marking pen and stitch running stitches for path lines and stem outline stitches for words.

5. Cut 1¼-inch strips from brown fabric and sew to center appliquéd piece. Cut 3½-inch strips from the print fabric and add to outside for borders. Stitch medium red rickrack in center of brown border.

6. Layer top, batting, and backing together and quilt as desired. Cut strips from red stripe fabric for binding and sew around outside edge of piece to complete the project.

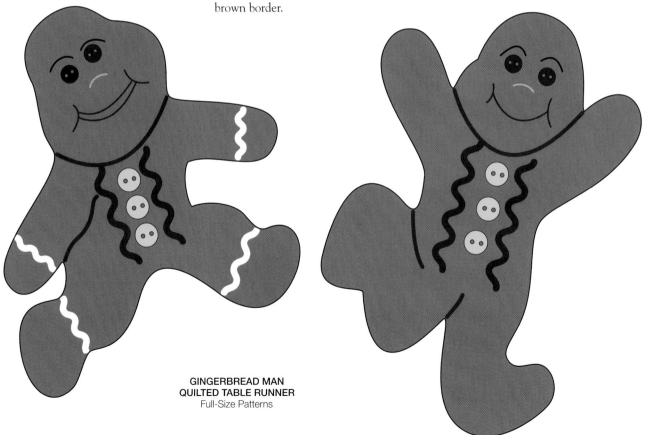

**GINGERBREAD MAN
QUILTED TABLE RUNNER**
Full-Size Patterns

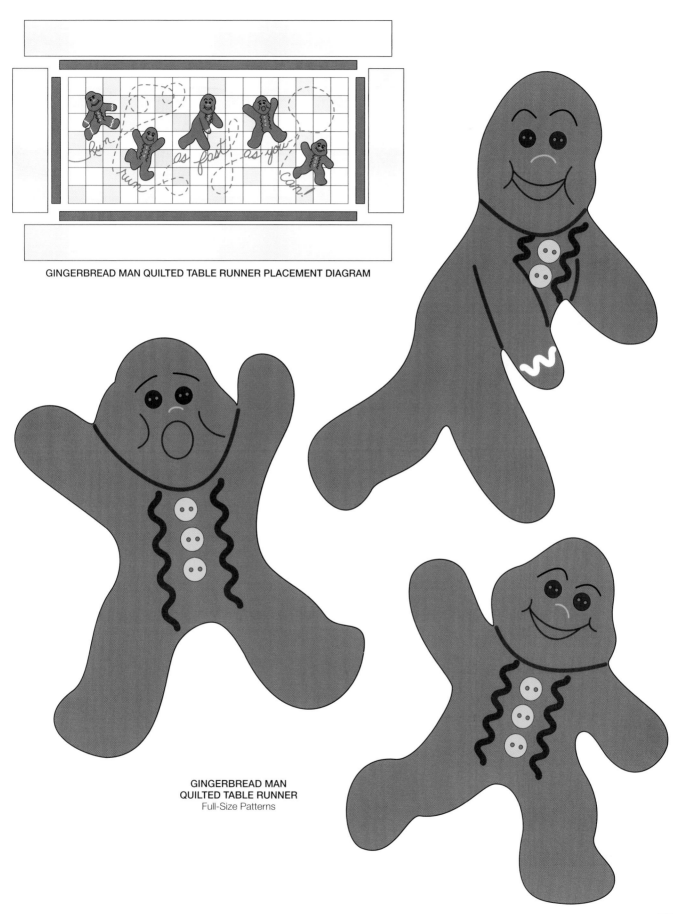

GINGERBREAD MAN QUILTED TABLE RUNNER PLACEMENT DIAGRAM

**GINGERBREAD MAN
QUILTED TABLE RUNNER**
Full-Size Patterns

Little Cook Apron
Shown on page 41

WHAT YOU NEED
One dish towel, approximately 16×26 inches (*Note:* This size towel makes an extra-small apron; for a larger apron, choose a larger towel)
One 12×12-inch dishcloth
4 yards ¾-inch-wide white twill tape
Matching threads

WHAT YOU DO
1. Measure approximately 11 inches up from bottom of towel; mark at sides. Fold the sides of towel to the back, starting at that mark and angling towel sides to form overlapping triangles. Fold top down 4 inches to the back. With matching thread, topstitch ¼ inch from outside along the side and top edges.
2. To make pocket, fold dishcloth in half. Place on center front of apron, 6 inches from bottom towel edge. With matching thread, stitch down center of dishcloth through towel. Cut a 12½-inch length of twill tape and stretch it horizontally across the dishcloth, wrapping tape over dish towel edges to the back. Pin at sides. Cut a 7½-inch length of twill tape. Place it over the center stitching line of the dishcloth, wrapping tape over dishcloth edges to the back. Pin in place at outside edges. Stitch around outside and bottom edges of dishcloth pocket over ribbon trim. Sew across top ribbon trim over center stitching line. Cut a 23-inch length of twill tape, tie into a bow, and tack with hand stitches from the back of the towel to attach to the intersecting ribbons on the pocket to complete the package look.

3. Cut two 26-inch lengths of twill tape for waist ties and two 20-inch lengths for neck ties. Tack neck ties at top edges by machine sewing through ribbon ends and towels. Tack waist ties at side edges just above pocket.

Mom's Festive Flounced Apron and Toddler's Apron
Shown on pages 40–41

WHAT YOU NEED
For Adult Apron:
Tracing paper; pencil
1½ yards of 45-inch-wide cotton polka-dot fabric
Matching thread; scissors

For Toddler's (size 3T) Apron:
Tracing paper; pencil
¾ yard cotton print fabric
5×7-inch scrap of red fabric for pocket
Matching thread; scissors

WHAT YOU DO
Cutting for Adult Apron: Enlarge and trace pattern pieces, *opposite*. Cut selvages off fabric and fold fabric in half lengthwise. Cut two 2-inch-wide strips the length of the fabric for waist ties. Cut one 1½-inch-wide strip the length of the fabric for neck binding and ties. Refold fabric in half lengthwise. Cut remaining pattern pieces.
Cutting for Toddler's Apron: Enlarge and trace pattern pieces, *page 52.* Cut two 2×36-inch strips for waist ties, cutting across the width of the fabric. Cut one 1½-inch-wide strip for the neck binding and ties, cutting across the width of the fabric. Cut remaining pattern pieces from print fabric. Cut two pocket pieces from contrasting red fabric.

To assemble:
For Adult Apron: With right sides together, stitch two pocket pieces together, stitching with a ½-inch seam around all edges, leaving a 4-inch opening for turning. Clip corners and curved edges. Turn right side out and press flat. Slip-stitch opening closed. Topstitch ¼ inch from side straight edges.

Fold apron in half and crease; do the same for pocket. Match fold lines and pin pocket in place on apron, 6 inches up from the bottom center of the apron. Edge-stitch around top and bottom edges of pocket through all layers. Sew a double row of stitching along center fold line of pocket through all layers.

Hem sides of apron by folding ¼ inch to the back twice. Stitch close to edge.

With right sides together, sew outer ruffle sections to center ruffle section at side straight seams, using ¼-inch seam. Narrow hem along outer edge of ruffle length by folding in ¼ inch twice and stitching close to outer edge or overcasting edge, folding ⅜ inch to the back and stitching close to overcast edge. Attach ruffle to bottom edge of apron, sewing ¼-inch seam and overcasting edges. Press seam toward apron and edge stitch close to seam line.

Press ¼ inch in on one short end of both neck ties. Press ¼ inch in on both long edges of neck tie, fold tie in half, and press. Find centers of tie and neck edge. With right sides together, pin one long edge of tie to neck edge, opening out the fold and stitching along that fold line with ¼-inch seam, starting and stopping at apron neck edges. Turn tie to the back and pin remaining folded edge over this seam. Stitch along long folded edges of entire tie length, from ends, on neck edge and continuing along remaining length to the end of the tie.

For waist ties, press ¼ inch in on one short end of both ties. Press ¼ inch in on both long sides, fold in half, and press. Stitch close to folded edges. Stitch waist ties at side edges of apron, just above the ruffle.

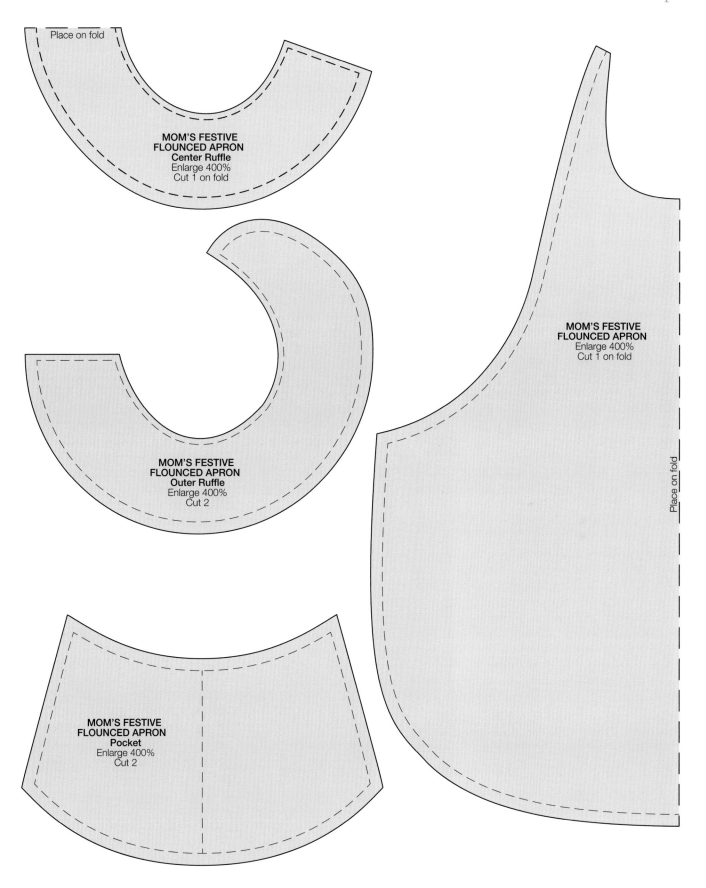

MOM'S FESTIVE
FLOUNCED APRON
Center Ruffle
Enlarge 400%
Cut 1 on fold

Place on fold

MOM'S FESTIVE
FLOUNCED APRON
Outer Ruffle
Enlarge 400%
Cut 2

MOM'S FESTIVE
FLOUNCED APRON
Enlarge 400%
Cut 1 on fold

Place on fold

MOM'S FESTIVE
FLOUNCED APRON
Pocket
Enlarge 400%
Cut 2

stitch it up!

For Child's Apron: For pocket, fold 1 inch to the wrong side on top straight edge. Press. Turn pocket facing back to the front side, folding on fold line marked on pattern. Stitch ¼ inch around outside edges of pockets from top edges and around lower curved edges. Turn facing to wrong side, fold under seam allowances along stitches, and press. Stitch close to edge of facing across top of pocket. Pin pocket to apron at placement marks and topstitch close to edges, reinforcing at top corners. Finish apron following instructions for adult apron, *page 50*.

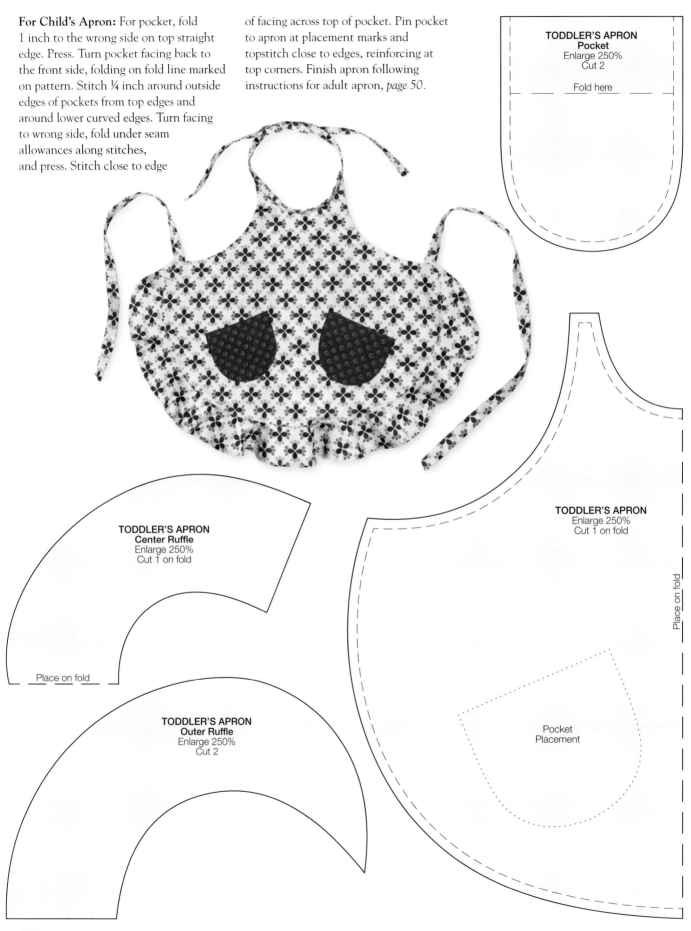

TODDLER'S APRON
Pocket
Enlarge 250%
Cut 2

Fold here

TODDLER'S APRON
Center Ruffle
Enlarge 250%
Cut 1 on fold

Place on fold

TODDLER'S APRON
Outer Ruffle
Enlarge 250%
Cut 2

TODDLER'S APRON
Enlarge 250%
Cut 1 on fold

Place on fold

Pocket
Placement

FELT GINGERBREAD TRIM 1
Full-Size Pattern

FELT GINGERBREAD TRIM 2
Full-Size Pattern

Felt Gingerbread Trims
Shown on page 42

**WHAT YOU NEED
FOR EACH ORNAMENT**
Tracing paper
Pencil
Two 6-inch squares felted
   wool for background
Five 2×2-inch scraps
   of felted wool for
   gingerbread figures
Matching sewing thread
Embroidery floss
15 tiny seed beads
Fabric glue

WHAT YOU DO
1. Trace patterns, *right* and *page 53*,
onto tracing paper and cut from
felted wool. *Note:* Felted wool
can be purchased at fabric stores.
For tips on felting your own wool,
see *page 159*.

Cut five gingerbread figures from contrasting color wool. Arrange gingerbread shapes onto background fabric according to layout shown.

2. Sew in place by hand or machine, with small buttonhole stitch in same thread color. Using two strands of contrasting embroidery floss, stitch zigzag lines across arms and legs, using a straight stitch. Make eyes using two strands of embroidery floss to stitch French knots. *Note:* For embroidery stitch diagrams see *page 159*.

3. Sew on tiny seed beads as button trim. Lay stitchery on background wool. Pin in place and cut out shape for backing. Using fabric glue, glue back to front. Using all strands of embroidery floss, make a hanging loop and stitch it between the two fabric layers.

Pretty Patchwork Pincushions
Shown on page 43

WHAT YOU NEED
4½-inch quilt squares pieced in desired colors (scraps of cotton fabrics) Pieced patterns shown are Amish Diamond, Shoofly, and Spinning Star
4½-inch-squares of cotton fabric for backing
Crushed walnut shells for stuffing
½ yard of ⅛-inch cording
Small buttons
Matching thread

WHAT YOU DO
1. Follow cutting and assembly instructions for desired quilt block, using ¼-inch seam allowances. Place quilt block right side together with backing square. Stitch around edges, leaving a small opening to turn. Clip corners, turn, and press.

2. Crease a piece of paper to make a funnel and pour walnut shells through opening until filled. Pin opening closed and hand-stitch together. Wrap cording around square, cross at back, and bring to front again. Tie in a tight knot at center front. Sew button over cording knot to complete.

FELT
GINGERBREAD
TRIM 1
Full-Size Pattern

FELT
GINGERBREAD
TRIM 2
Full-Size Pattern

**FELT GINGERBREAD TRIM 1
PLACEMENT DIAGRAM**

**FELT GINGERBREAD TRIM 2
PLACEMENT DIAGRAM**

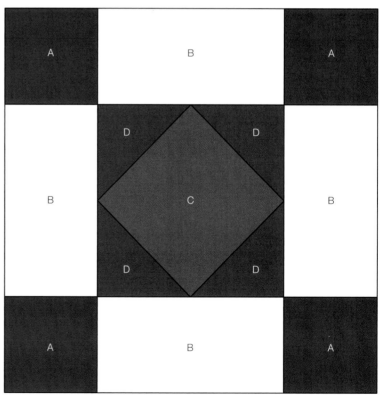

PRETTY PATCHWORK PINCUSHIONS
Amish Diamond Block Pattern

Amish Diamond
Add D pieces to 2 opposite sides of C, then to 2 remaining sides. Add B pieces to 2 sides of CD unit. Add A to each end of B (2 times); add AB units to each side of the first section to make the block.

Shoofly
Make BB unit (4 times). Join A pieces with BB units to form rows, referring to the diagram. Join rows to form the block.

Spinning Star
Sew AB unit (4 times). Join the units into 2 rows, then join the rows to make the block.

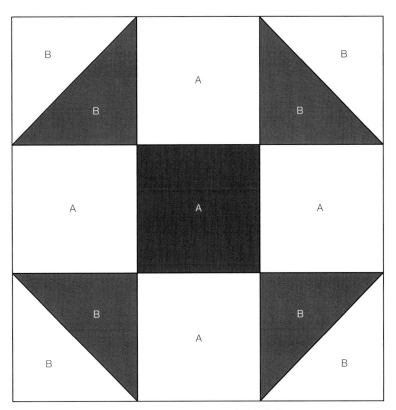

PRETTY PATCHWORK PINCUSHIONS
Shoofly Block Pattern

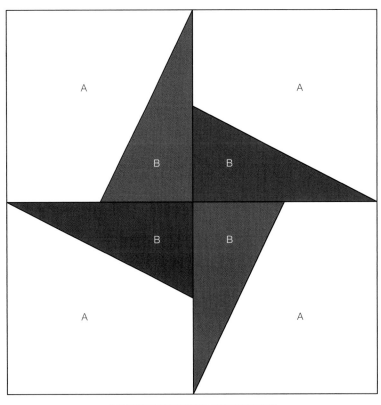

PRETTY PATCHWORK PINCUSHIONS
Spinning Star Block Pattern

55

Winter Woolen Birds

Shown on page 44

WHAT YOU NEED
Tracing paper; pencil; marking pen
Scraps of wool fabric
Matching sewing thread
Embroidery floss
Small amount Poly-fil fiberfill
Nylon thread
Artificial berries or greenery (optional)

WHAT YOU DO
1. Enlarge and trace pattern pieces, *below,* onto tracing paper and cut out. Cut shapes from wool fabrics. Use ¼-inch seam allowance for all stitching. With right sides together, stitch around outside and lower edges of main body pieces, starting and stopping at points marked on patterns. Clip corners and curves, and turn right side out.
2. With right sides together, stitch one side of tummy piece to side of main body. Lightly stuff the body with Poly-fil. Turn tummy piece over and handstitch to main body piece.

3. Mark stitching lines on wing pieces and use three strands embroidery floss to work stem stitch details on wings. With right sides together, stitch wings together, leaving an opening for turning. Clip corners and curves, and turn right side out. Handstitch opening closed. Stitch wings in place on main body section by

taking a few invisible handstitches beneath wing and into body section. Using six strands embroidery floss, make French knots for eyes. *Note:* For embroidery stitch diagrams, see *page 159.* Sew nylon thread through top for a hanger. Add berries or greenery at beak, if desired, and stitch in place.

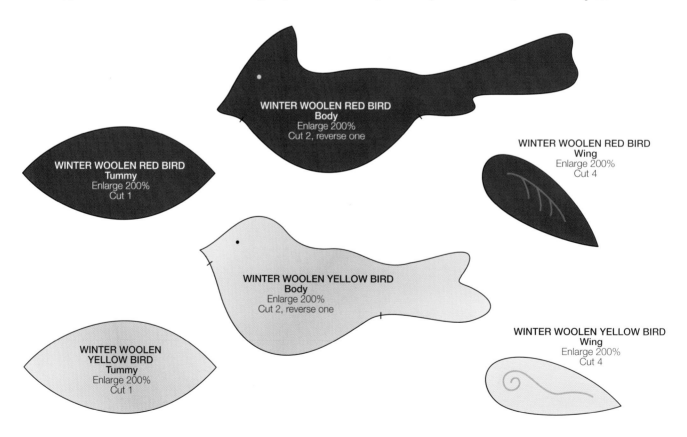

WINTER WOOLEN RED BIRD
Body
Enlarge 200%
Cut 2, reverse one

WINTER WOOLEN RED BIRD
Tummy
Enlarge 200%
Cut 1

WINTER WOOLEN RED BIRD
Wing
Enlarge 200%
Cut 4

WINTER WOOLEN YELLOW BIRD
Body
Enlarge 200%
Cut 2, reverse one

WINTER WOOLEN
YELLOW BIRD
Tummy
Enlarge 200%
Cut 1

WINTER WOOLEN YELLOW BIRD
Wing
Enlarge 200%
Cut 4

CLASSIC COUNTRY STOCKING
Enlarge 200%
Cut 2 fabric, reversing one
Cut 2 lining, reversing one
(add ¼" seam allowance)

CLASSIC COUNTRY STOCKING Gift Tag
Enlarge 200%
Cut 2

Country Classic Stocking

Shown on page 45

WHAT YOU NEED

Tracing paper; pencil; scissors
½ yard red toile print cotton fabric
½ yard tan cotton fabric for lining
16×11-inch piece of tan fabric for outside cuff
Two 12×20-inch pieces cotton batting
Red sewing thread
Tan sewing thread
Red embroidery floss
Water-soluble marking pen
Awl tool

WHAT YOU DO

1. Enlarge and trace patterns, *above*, and cut out. Cut two 12×20-inch pieces of toile fabric and two lining fabric pieces inches. Layer batting between print and lining pieces. Quilt around shapes in print, using matching red sewing thread. Use patterns to cut stocking front and back pieces. With right sides together, stitch stocking pieces together around side and lower edges, using a ¼-inch seam. Overcast edges to finish seam.

2. For pleated cuff, cut tan fabric to 15¾×10½ inches. Press creases along length of cuff piece with the first crease 1¼ inches from the top edge and every inch thereafter. Sew along each folded edge, ⅜ inch along pressed edges, making nine even folds. Press folds flat, hiding stitching lines. Cut a piece of tan lining fabric to 15¾×4 inches for the cuff facing. Stitch short ends of cuff pieces together with ½-inch seam allowances. With right sides together, stitch lining to cuff along bottom edge, using ¼-inch seam. Clip seam, turn, and press. Baste top edges together.

3. From the toile fabric, cut a 2×8-inch strip for the hanger. With right sides together, fold strip in half lengthwise and sew along long edge using a ¼-inch seam. Turn right side out and press. Fold length in half and align top edges of hanger even with top edge of stocking at side seam, having fold extend down into stocking. Baste across top. Slip cuff inside quilted stocking, right side of cuff to wrong side of stocking and top raw edges even. Sew around top edges using ½-inch seam.

Turn cuff over to outside of stocking. Press top edge of cuff along first pleat sewing line.

4. To make identifying tag: Trace pattern and cut out. Cut two pieces of tan fabric and one piece of batting from pattern. On front of one tan piece, write name with water-soluble marking pen, centered on tag. Stitch name along marking lines, using three strands embroidery floss to make running stitches and French knot for the dot. *Note:* For embroidery stitch diagrams, see *page 159*. Place tag front and back right sides together and layer batting on back. Stitch around side and pointed ends, leaving short flat end open for turning. Clip batting close to stitching lines, clip corners, turn, and press. Hand-stitch opening closed. Press flat. Make eyelet or small buttonhole in point. Use awl tool to make a hole or clip center of buttonhole. Thread length of 6-strand embroidery floss through hole, thread through hanging loop, and knot ends together.

Welcome your guests with handmade wreaths and decorate your table with stunning centerpieces that all say "Merry Christmas."

festive wreaths
& centerpieces

Mismatched vases topped with red carnations create stunning **Red Carnation Topiaries**, *opposite*. Greenery and bells of Ireland tied with apple-green ribbon create **Winter Green Swags**, *opposite*. Round candles, dripped with crayon wax and sprinkled with tiny beads, make a **Shimmering Candle Arrangement**, *above*. Sugared cranberries surround the pretty candles. Instructions begin on page 66.

Fresh plums are sugared and stacked on bits of fresh rosemary for a lovely **Sugar Plum Centerpiece,** *right.* Tuck sugared candies in similar hues around the fruit and herbs for a fresh and colorful arrangement. Instructions are on page 66.

A classic-shape glass vase becomes a favorite centerpiece in so many ways. Top with a pretty plate and candles for a **Plated Centerpiece**, *above left*. To make a **Cranberry Centerpiece**, *above right*, fill the vase with cranberries and a red candle. **Holly and Roses Arrangement**, *left*, showcases beautiful roses floating in water with a holly crown at the base. Instructions are on page 67.

Transform a footed glass serving piece and fresh blooms into a tabletop focal point by creating a **Flower and Berry Arrangement**, *below left.* Capture the natural beauty of key limes by making a **Limelight Centerpiece**, *below right.* Instructions are on page 67.

Acorn crowns add interesting texture and color when they combine to make a **Natural Beauty Wreath**, *above*. A welcoming bird finishes the look. Instructions are on page 68.

Shape honeycomb wax into a bow to decorate a **Holiday Gift Candle**, *left*.

Display a seldom-used scarf beautifully by swaddling it around a wreath form to

make a **Wrapped-Up Wreath**, *above*. For a little extra sparkle, add a vintage

pin near the fringe. Instructions are on pages 68–69.

Crisscross peppermint sticks around a golden candle for a **Good as Gold Centerpiece,** *above.* Wrap red, green, and gold textured yarn around several sizes of foam balls and then glue them to a wreath form to make a **Warm Winter Wreath,** *left.* Instructions are on page 69.

Red Carnation Topiaries

Shown on page 58

WHAT YOU NEED

Three 12- to 14-inch-tall white vases
    in similar shapes
Three 4- to 6-inch round florist's foam
    balls, such as Oasis
Small pail; water; flat tray or plate
Fresh red carnations—approximately
    3 dozen for each topiary
Apple green votive candles and holders

WHAT YOU DO

1. Measure the vases and check the size
of the florist's foam. For each topiary, soak
florist foam in a pail of water until moist.
Working with one ball at a time, lay the
moist ball on tray or plate.
2. Clip blooms from carnations, leaving
about a 1½-inch stem. Poke the stem
end into the moist ball until the top
two-thirds of the ball is covered. Place
in vase to check size. Only the part that
is showing needs to be covered with the
carnations. Repeat with remaining two
balls. Set carnations in vases. Set candles
in holders and place around vases.
Never leave a burning candle unattended.

Winter Green Swags

Shown on page 58

Bells of Ireland stems
Crafts wire; wire cutters
Pine boughs approximately
    18 inches long
4 yards of 3-inch-wide apple green ribbon

WHAT YOU DO

Wire three or four bells of Ireland stems
and pieces of pine boughs together at
one end. Form a wire hanging loop on
the back side. Cut the ribbon in half.
Tie a bow with each section of ribbon.
Wire to the top of the swag.

Shimmering Candle Arrangement

Shown on page 59

WHAT YOU NEED

2 light green ball-style candles
Aluminum foil
Taper candle
Match
Dark red crayons
Mini beads
Small clear glass dish
Fresh cranberries
White granulated sugar

WHAT YOU DO

Place the candles on the aluminum foil.
Light the taper candle and place the
crayon into the flame letting the wax
drip onto the ball candle, starting at the
top of the ball candle and letting the wax
drip down the sides. After the desired
effect is achieved, immediately sprinkle
with mini beads. Allow the wax and
beads to dry. Set the candles in the
dish and surround with cranberries.
Sprinkle the cranberries with sugar.
Never leave a burning candle unattended.

Sugar Plum Centerpiece

Shown on page 60

WHAT YOU NEED

Fresh red plums
Fresh rosemary
Aluminum foil
Dried egg whites such as Just Whites
Water; paintbrush
Granulated sugar
Glass cake stand
Sugared hard candies

WHAT YOU DO

1. Wash and dry the plums and
rosemary and place on the foil. Mix the
dried egg whites following manufacturer's
instructions. You will need about ½ cup
of the mixture. Use a paintbrush to
brush the mixture on the plums and
rosemary. Sprinkle with sugar. Allow to
dry about 30 minutes. Turn plums and
herbs over and repeat on the other side.
Allow to dry. *Note:* Sugar will become
hard and shiny.
2. Arrange the sugared plums and
rosemary on cake stand, tucking rosemary
between the plums. Add sugared candies
around the base of the arrangement.

Three-with-One Centerpieces

Shown on page 61

For Holly and Roses Arrangement:

Set the glass vase on a clear glass bowl or plate. Fill the vase with water, greenery, and freshly cut rose blooms. Add cut bits of holly around the vase on the plate.

For Plated Centerpiece:

Fill the vase with silver pinecones and silver and green jingle bells. Set a glass plate on top of the vase and set three green votives on the plate.

Never leave a burning candle unattended.

For Cranberry Centerpiece:

Center a red candle in the vase. Surround the candle with fresh cranberries. Set the vase on a clear glass plate and surround with vintage Christmas ornaments.

Never leave a burning candle unattended.

Flower and Berry Arrangement

Shown on page 62

WHAT YOU NEED

Florist's foam, such as Oasis
White place mat
10-inch diameter clear bowl
2 bags of fresh cranberries
Stems of paperwhite flowers
Fresh greenery
White pillar candles
26-gauge gold craft wire

WHAT YOU DO

1. Place the florist's foam into a 10-inch-diameter bowl centered on the place mat. Cover with cranberries. Secure about two dozen paperwhites into the cranberry-covered foam. Add more cranberries. *Note:* To grow your own paperwhites, buy paperwhite bulbs about eight weeks before you plan to display the blooms and force them to grow by placing the bulbs in a shallow pan of water.

2. Tuck greenery and a few more paperwhites around the bowl. String cranberries onto gold wire to wrap around the white pillar candles. Surround the berry-filled container with the candles.

Never leave a burning candle unattended.

Limelight Centerpiece

Shown on page 62

WHAT YOU NEED

Large covered glass canister
Distilled water
Fresh key limes; fresh limes
Sharp knife

WHAT YOU DO

Be sure the jar is clean and dry. Fill the jar two-thirds full with distilled water. Slice some of the limes. Very carefully add the slices and whole limes to the water, adding water if necessary to fill the jar nearly to the top. Replace the top on jar.

Natural Beauty Wreath

Shown on page 63

WHAT YOU NEED

10-inch plastic foam flat wreath form
Acorn tops (about 100)
   (see Sources, *page 159*)
Hot-glue gun
Hot-glue sticks
Purchased artificial bird
2 yards of ½-inch-wide twine

WHAT YOU DO

Lay foam wreath on a protected surface.
Sort acorn tops by size. Use the hot-glue
gun and hot glue to attach the acorn tops
to the wreath form. Use larger ones first,
filling in with smaller ones. Allow to dry.

Glue the bird to the inner side of the
wreath. Tie a twine bow and glue at the
top of the wreath.

Holiday Gift Candle

Shown on page 64

WHAT YOU NEED

Tracing paper
Pencil
Red honeycomb beeswax sheets
Crafts knife
Red candle glitter
Hair dryer
5×6-inch red pillar candle

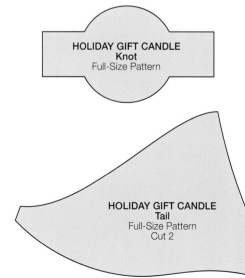

HOLIDAY GIFT CANDLE
Knot
Full-Size Pattern

HOLIDAY GIFT CANDLE
Tail
Full-Size Pattern
Cut 2

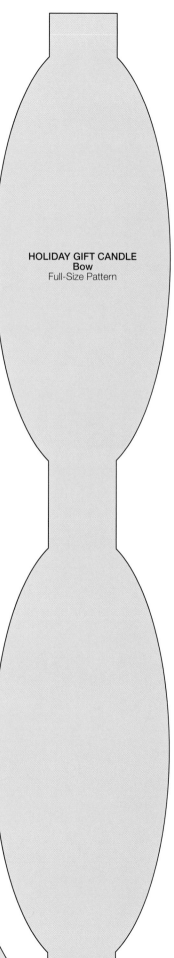

HOLIDAY GIFT CANDLE
Bow
Full-Size Pattern

WHAT YOU DO

Trace the patterns, *opposite*; cut out the shapes. Lay the pattern pieces on beeswax and use a crafts knife to cut around the shapes, cutting one bow, one bow knot, and two bow tails. Refer to the photo, *opposite, bottom left*. *Note:* The bow is shaped in the photo; the long strip wraps around the purchased candle.

Lay the bow piece flat and bring each end in to overlap at the center. Press in place and cover the bow with glitter. Wrap the bow knot around the center of the bow, molding the knot into shape. Slightly overlap and press together the narrow ends of the bow tails. Cover them with glitter. Press the parts of the bow together, using a hair dryer to warm the wax to make it slightly tacky. Coat the bow with glitter.

Cut a 1⅜-inch-wide strip of beeswax long enough to reach around the pillar. Press the bow on the center of the strip. Cover the band with glitter. Wrap the strip around the candle, using the hair dryer to firmly attach the strip to the candle if necessary.
Never leave a burning candle unattended.

Wrapped-Up Wreath
Shown on page 64

WHAT YOU NEED
12-inch round-edge foam wreath form
Long lightweight scarf with fringe such as a printed pashmina woven scarf
Straight pins
Greenery; brooch

WHAT YOU DO
Lay the wreath form on a flat surface. Fold the scarf in half lengthwise making it narrower. Pin one scarf end to the foam wreath form. Wrap the scarf around the form pinning as necessary. Wrap until the fringe end folds over the top of the wreath. Pin greenery and brooch on the scarf.

Good as Gold Centerpiece
Shown on page 65

WHAT YOU NEED
Gold metallic candle
Clear glass plate
Peppermint sticks
Gold fabric

WHAT YOU DO
Be sure the plate is clean and dry. Place the candle on the center of the plate. Break the candy sticks to surround the candle, layering the sticks. Place the arrangement on the gold fabric.
Never leave a burning candle unattended.

Warm Winter Wreath
Shown on page 65

WHAT YOU NEED
Plastic foam balls, such as Styrofoam in a variety of sizes (about 25)
1 skein each green, gold, and red nubby yarn
Straight pins
12-inch plastic foam wreath
Hot-glue sticks
Hot-glue gun

WHAT YOU DO
1. Plan the arrangement of the balls and choose the desired sizes. Choose the desired color of yarn and wrap the foam balls with the yarn until completely covered. Tuck the yarn end under the last wrap and pin or hot-glue in place. Set aside wrapped foam balls.
2. Use the green yarn to wrap the entire plastic foam wreath. Pin or hot-glue in place. Tie a piece of yarn around the top of the wrapped wreath for a hanger.
3. Beginning with larger balls and filling in with smaller ones, glue the covered balls onto the covered wreath. Let dry.

Return to the beauty and elegance of Christmases long ago by re-creating vintage embellishments that are as endearing now as they were then.

christmas
past

Full of Christmas charm, this magnificent tree is decorated with dozens of vintage-style trims. Start by making **Layered Silk Flowerettes**, *above*, using circles of silk and centers of tulle or fabric stickers. Then make **Starburst Ornaments**, **Vintage Jewelry Trims**, **Tulle Candy Bags**, and **Pretty Paper Purses** to adorn the glorious tree. Fresh orange slices are hung from narrow ribbons, and sheer ribbons fall from the citrus tree topper. Turn the page to see the trims up close for this festive tree. Instructions are on pages 80–82.

Beautifully simple to make, **Starburst Ornaments**, *above*, combine fine glitter with a single jewel. A vintage earring or brooch tops the ribbon that holds **Vintage Jewelry Trims**, *above right* and *right*. Instructions are on page 81.

Fold papers of all textures and colors to make **Pretty Paper Purses**, *left*. Attach a tiny jewel or piece of jewelry for a fastener and a satin ribbon for the strap. Sew gold tulle into small bags and fill with old-fashioned candy to make **Tulle Candy Bags**, *below*. Layer silk and then add coiled tulle for the center to create another version of **Layered Silk Flowerettes**, *below left*. Instructions are on pages 81–82.

Purchased cut-out paper borders and a shiny bright ball trim are all it takes to make simply stunning **Beautfiul Border Trims**, *above*. Fabric prints from the 1930s are the secret to making the **Vintage Feed Sack Stockings**, *opposite*. The reproduction fabrics come from designs often seen on feed sacks that were saved to sew into quilts or garments. The muslin cuffs are quilted with simple stitches. Instructions and patterns are on pages 82–83.

Vintage red cookie cutters surround a red candle for a Cookie Cutter

Centerpiece, *above left*, that flickers with red Christmas light.

The 1950s and 1960s introduced a new type of tree made from aluminum.

These bright and shiny trees were often decorated with Yarn Pom-Poms,

above right, and bright ball ornaments. Instructions are on page 84.

Some of the most detailed holiday motifs from the 1960s are found on greeting cards. Search antiques stores for the ones you like, then add some glue and glitter to make Sparkling Vintage Greetings, *below.* Instructions are on page 85.

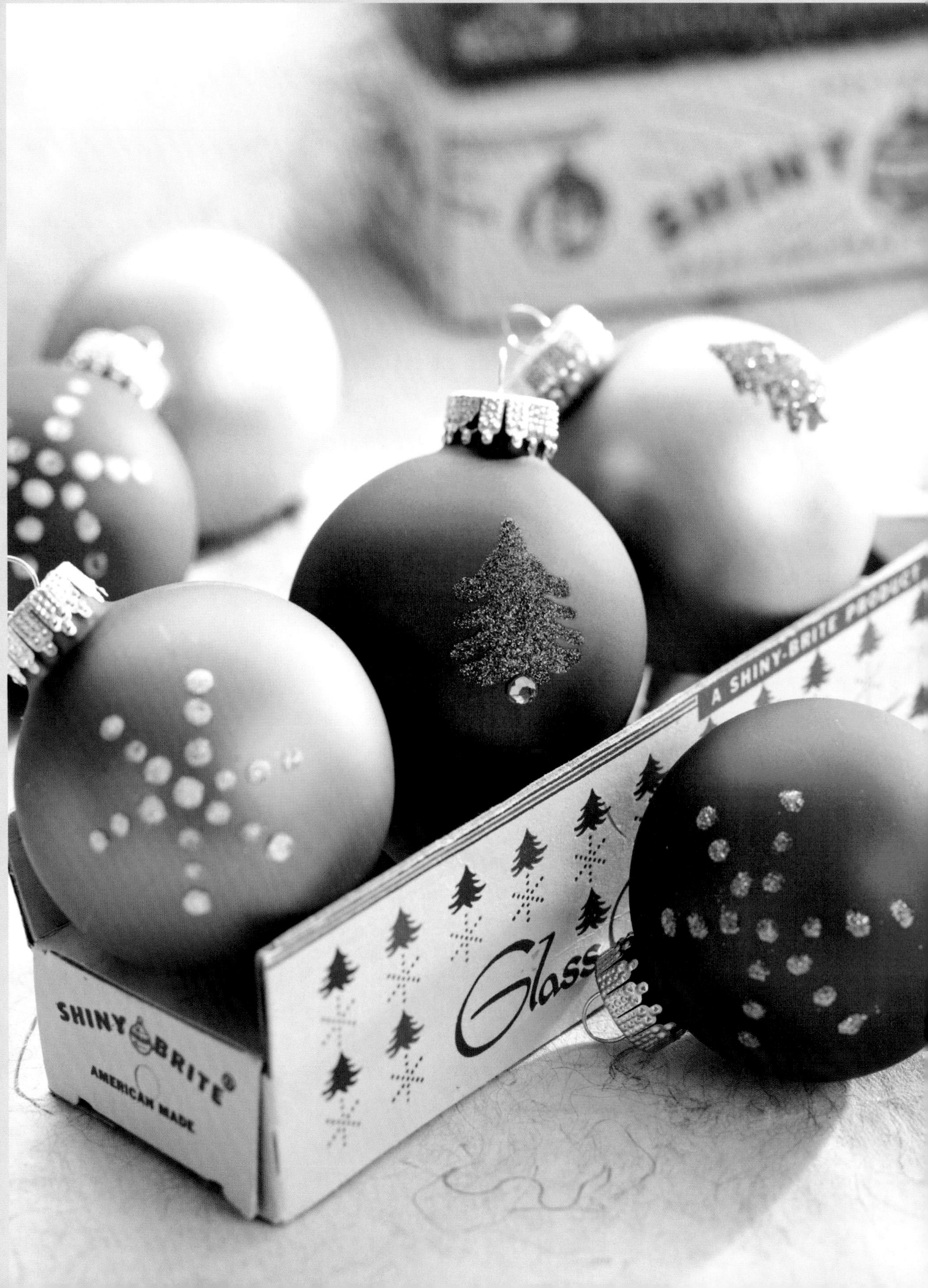
A SHINY-BRITE PRODUCT
Glass
SHINY BRITE
AMERICAN MADE

Clever holiday patterns can be found on vintage ornament boxes. Repeat the patterns to make **Simple Motif Trims**, *opposite*, for your ornaments today. Search for antique postcards to use for **Postcard Greetings**, *above*, for all those special people on your Christmas list. Instructions are on page 85.

Layered Silk Flowerettes

Shown on pages 70, 71, 73

WHAT YOU NEED
FOR ONE FLOWERETTE

Tracing paper; pencil

2 8-inch squares of pure silk or
    silk shantung in solid or
    printed colors

Scissors; candle; match

Bowl of water

Custard or oven-safe cup

Cookie sheet

Fabric glue; glitter

¼ yard gold tulle or floral
    fabric sticker

Crafts glue

Fine glitter to match or coordinate
    with fabrics

Narrow ribbon for hanging

WHAT YOU DO

1. Trace and enlarge patterns, *below*. Cut 2 circles from the silk print or solid colors: Cut one 5-inch circle and one 3½-inch circle. Fill the bowl with water. Set the candle on the cookie sheet. Light the candle and very carefully and quickly move the edge of each of the circles through the flame to seal the edges. See Photo A. *Note:* Some silks burn more than others. Always have water nearby in case of fire. After sealing the edges of the silk, dip the entire piece into the bowl of water.

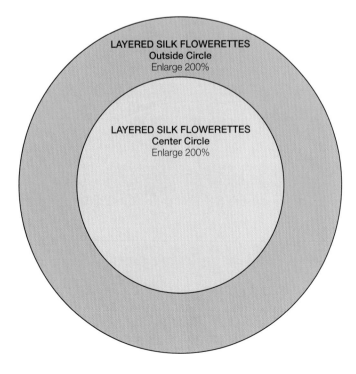

LAYERED SILK FLOWERETTES
Outside Circle
Enlarge 200%

LAYERED SILK FLOWERETTES
Center Circle
Enlarge 200%

See Photo B. Drape over the oven-safe cup. See Photo C. Place in a 200°F oven for about 10 minutes or until dry. Remove from the oven and cool.

2. Run a narrow line of crafts glue around the edges of both pieces of silk. Dust with glitter. Allow to dry.

3. Use fabric glue to adhere the small piece of silk inside the larger one. Cut a small square of tulle and glue to the center. Decorate the center by placing a fabric sticker in the center or rolling a piece of tulle to glue to the center. Glue a fine ribbon on the back for hanging.

Starburst Ornaments
Shown on pages 70, 72

WHAT YOU NEED
Pastel ball-style ornament
Crafts glue
Toothpick
Fine silver glitter
Jewel in contrasting color

WHAT YOU DO
Be sure the ornament is clean and dry. Use a toothpick to spread crafts glue into a large starburst shape, pulling the glue from a center spot. Dust with glitter. Glue a jewel to the center of the glittered star. Let dry. Repeat on other sides of the ornament. Let dry.

Vintage Jewelry Trims
Shown on pages 70, 72

WHAT YOU NEED
Pastel ornaments
Vintage-style stickers
Jewel stickers to match ornament color
10 inches of ¼-inch-wide sheer ribbon
Single vintage earring or brooch

WHAT YOU DO
Be sure ornament is clean and dry. Position the sticker on the front of the ornament. Press the jewels above and below the sticker. Thread the ribbon through the top and tie at top and again about 3 inches above first tie. To secure to tree, clip the earring or pin the brooch to the tree over the ribbon.

Pretty Paper Purses
Shown on pages 70, 73

WHAT YOU NEED
Tracing paper; pencil
Scissors
6×3-inch piece of scrapbook paper
    in desired color and texture
8 inches of ¼-inch-wide ribbon
Crafts glue
Vintage button or large jewel

WHAT YOU DO
Trace desired purse pattern, *page 82,* onto tracing paper and cut out. Trace around scrapbook paper and cut out. Fold along flap line. Tuck and glue ribbon inside front flap and glue flap to purse front. Adhere button or jewel to front flap.

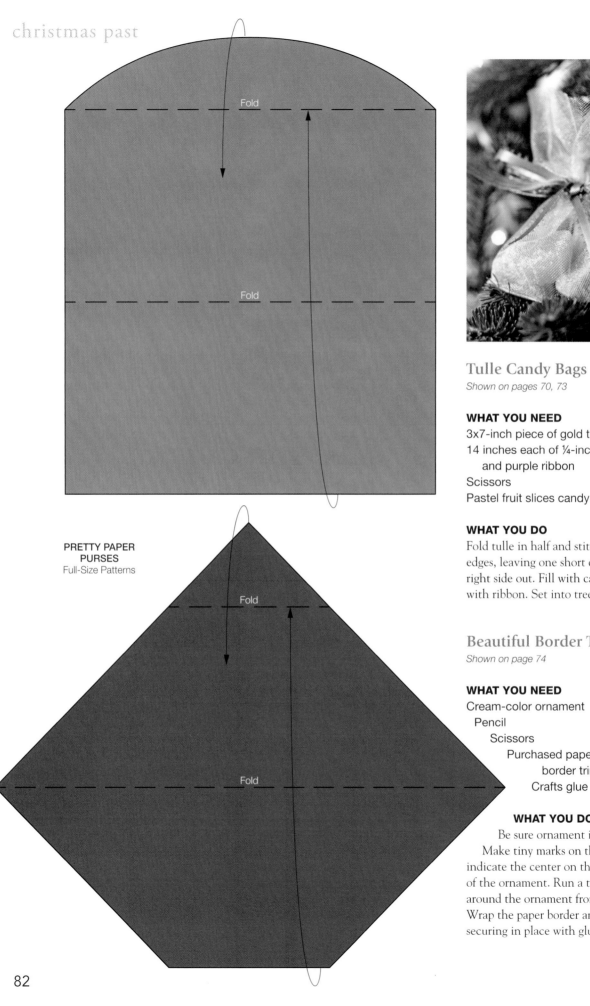

Fold

Fold

PRETTY PAPER PURSES
Full-Size Patterns

Fold

Fold

Tulle Candy Bags
Shown on pages 70, 73

WHAT YOU NEED
3x7-inch piece of gold tulle
14 inches each of ¼-inch-wide blue
 and purple ribbon
Scissors
Pastel fruit slices candy

WHAT YOU DO
Fold tulle in half and stitch around three edges, leaving one short edge open. Turn right side out. Fill with candies and tie with ribbon. Set into tree branches.

Beautiful Border Trims
Shown on page 74

WHAT YOU NEED
Cream-color ornament
 Pencil
  Scissors
   Purchased paper scrapbook
    border trims
    Crafts glue

WHAT YOU DO
Be sure ornament is clean and dry. Make tiny marks on the ornament to indicate the center on the front and back of the ornament. Run a tiny line of glue around the ornament from front to back. Wrap the paper border around the trim, securing in place with glue.

Vintage Feed Sack Stockings

Shown on page 75

WHAT YOU NEED

Tracing paper; pencil
Scissors
Fabric in desired colors (we used
    1930s feed sack-print fabrics)
¼ yard iron-on fleece
¼ yard lining fabric
⅛ yard desired fabric for cuff
¼-inch-wide solid-color piping
Threads to match fabrics

WHAT YOU DO

1. Enlarge and trace the patterns, *right*, onto tracing paper. Cut out the patterns. With right sides of stocking fabric together, cut two stocking shapes, adding ¼-inch seam allowances on all sides and ½-inch seam allowance at the top. Cut two pieces of iron-on fleece the same size. Cut two lining pieces without adding ¼-inch seam allowances. For loop, cut a 2×6-inch piece of fabric.

2. Press fleece to the wrong side of each stocking. Baste piping to edge of stocking front. Sew stocking pieces together, right sides together, being careful not to catch piping in the seam. Clip curves; turn right side out. Press. Stitch lining together with right sides together using a ¼-inch seam. Clip curves. Turn; insert lining inside stocking. Baste across top of lining and stocking ½ inch from stocking top.

3. For loop, fold long edges of fabric into the center and in half again to make a ½×60-inch piece. Stitch close to fold. Fold in half with top raw edges even. Place loop inside lining of stocking and baste to top edge of stocking.

4. For small stocking cuff, fold cuff fabric in half right sides together; place cuff pattern on fold as indicated on pattern. Cut out 2 cuff pieces, leaving ¼-inch seam allowances at cuff sides and ½-inch seam allowance at top. From pattern, cut one fleece cuff piece without adding seam allowances. Cut along fold line, making two pieces. Press fleece to back of each cuff fabric, covering only half of each cuff. Machine- or hand-quilt the cuff. Open cuff; with right sides together, stitch the sides of the cuff with ¼-inch seams. Fold cuff in half to form a ring. Put cuff inside stocking with top raw edges even and right side of cuff facing lining. Stitch top together with ½-inch seam. Turn cuff to outside over stocking. Press.

**VINTAGE FEED SACK
STOCKING CUFF**
Enlarge 200%
Cut 2

Place on fold

**VINTAGE FEED SACK
STOCKING**
Enlarge 200%
Cut 2 from fabric, reversing 1
Cut 2 from lining, reversing 1

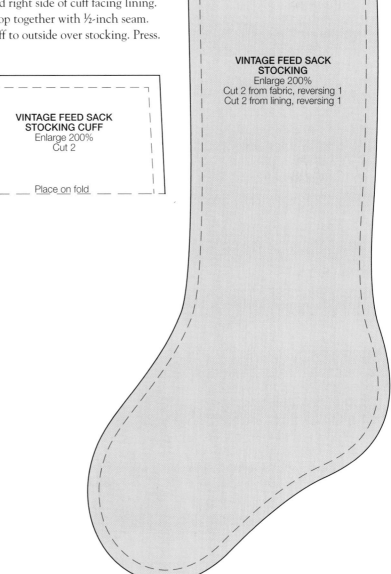

Cookie Cutter Centerpiece
Shown on page 76

WHAT YOU NEED
Low glass bowl
Candle in glass container
Vintage red cookie cutters
White garland

WHAT YOU DO
Be sure the bowl is clean and dry. Place
the candle in the center of the bowl.
Arrange the garland around the candle.
Place cookie cutters on the garland.
Never leave a burning candle unattended.

Yarn Pom-Poms
Shown on page 76

WHAT YOU NEED
4 yards white cotton yarn
10-inch length of cotton yarn
Scissors

WHAT YOU DO
Wrap the 4 yards of yarn around four
fingers about 80 times. Yarn will seem
thick. Remove from hand and place on
table. Carefully tie the 10-inch piece of
yarn around the center. See Photo A.
Use scissors to cut all of the loops at both
sides. See Photo B. Pull all of the cut yarn
toward one side, shaking to combine yarn.
See Photo C. Use scissors to shape the
pom-pom. See Photo D.

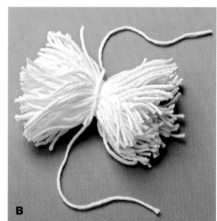

A

B

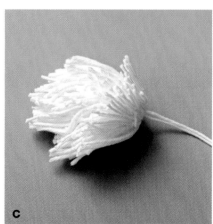

C

D

Sparkling Vintage Greetings
Shown on page 77

WHAT YOU NEED
Vintage Christmas cards or
   reproduction cards available at
   antiques stores or flea markets
Crafts glue
Paintbrush
Fine glitter in desired color
Paper punch (optional)
Fine ribbon (optional)

WHAT YOU DO
Choose desired card and decide which
areas to embellish with glitter. Look for
white areas such as the beard, mustache,
and pom-pom on Santa images or or
snow on trees. Choose areas such as veins
on flowers or leaves. Use the paintbrush
to brush glue on the chosen areas to
embellish. Dust with glitter. Allow to dry.
If desired, punch a hole in the corner for
hanging and add a fine ribbon.

Simple Motif Trims
Shown on page 78

WHAT YOU NEED
Red, green, and gold ball-style
   ornaments
Pencil
Crafts glue
Green and gold glitter
Gold jewel

WHAT YOU DO
For the Tree Ornament: Referring to
the photo and the pattern, *opposite*, mark
where the tree is to be placed using a
pencil. Using the bottle of glue, make the
lines of the tree. Dust with green glitter.
Allow to dry. Glue a jewel at the base for
the trunk. Allow to dry.
For the Snowflake Ornament: Referring
to the photo and the pattern, *right*, mark
where the snowflake is to be placed using
a pencil. Using the bottle of glue, make
small dots on the ornament. Dust with
gold glitter. Allow to dry.

Postcard Greetings
Shown on page 79

WHAT YOU NEED
Cardstock in desired color
Vintage or reproduction vintage
   postcards (see Sources, *page 159*)
Pencil; scissors; paper punch
Narrow ribbon

WHAT YOU DO
1. For each card, cut two pieces of
cardstock to measure about ½ to 1 inch
larger than the vintage card being used.
Punch two holes or a series of holes in the
two pieces of cardstock along the left side.
Center and glue the card to the front piece.
2. Run a thin line of glue around the
card and dust with glitter. Allow to dry.
Place the pieces together and thread a
ribbon through the holes, tying a bow
at the top or at the side to secure.

SIMPLE MOTIF TRIMS
Full-Size Pattern

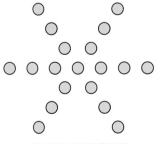

SIMPLE MOTIF TRIMS
Full-Size Pattern

*Handmade gifts are the dearest of all—so create
something special for everyone on your Chrismtas list.*

SIMPLE GIFTS &
clever wraps

A simple cookie cutter stands tall on a **Dressed-Up Tree Wrap**, *above*,

assembled in minutes. Fill in the cutter with bright green premade bows.

Every little girl loves mittens, so knit a pair or two of **Embellished**

Knitted Mittens, *opposite*, for those little ladies on your holiday list.

After the simple knitting is done, add embellishments to personalize

each pair. Instructions are on pages 96–97.

Choose a favorite bead to showcase with sterling silver bobbles to make a **Beaded Silver Necklace**, *above*. Tear pieces of cranberry-pink scrapbook paper and dip them in watercolor paint to make a **Paper Rose Topper**, *right*. Instructions for the projects are on pages 97–98.

Printed scrapbook paper is easily scored and folded to hold holiday secrets. Make these **Holiday Surprise Holders**, *above*, using a color scheme to match the gift. A little purse with a golden handle holds a special gift inside. Make the **Gifty Purse Card**, *left*, using stickers, paper, and trims. Instructions are on pages 98–99.

Discontinued sewing patterns, often sold for a few cents at fabric stores, contain sturdy printed tissue. To save money, or for that seamstress on your list, create **Pattern Wraps** and **Tissue Bows**, *top*, that feature not only the tissue wrap but also bits of rickrack and buttons. **Printed Fabric Wraps**, *bottom*, are a clever way to wrap hard-to-wrap gifts. Choose a holiday print in colors that coordinate with the gift inside the wrap. Instructions are on pages 99–100.

A plain-Jane glass jar becomes a lovely gift when it is painted with easy-to-find glass paints to make a **Candy Stripe Jar**, *above left*. **Monogrammed Handkerchieves**, *above right*, are an easy and much-appreciated gift for the men on your gift list. Each piece works up quickly with any color of embroidery floss. Instructions and patterns are on pages 100–101.

Want to make sure your gifts are perfect for everyone on your list? Make **Personalized Container Gifts**, *opposite*, that are sure to please. For the chef in the group, make a **Basket in Black and White** filled with specialty salts and peppers. Any seamstress will love a **Sewing Basket** full of essential notions. An **Old-Fashioned Basket** contains sarsaparilla and Christmas candies. Fill a red colander with a variety of cranberry products to make a **Cranberry Goodie Basket**.

Let the beautiful texture and shape of nature dictate your package trims. Acorn tops with a jingle bell tucked inside make a delightful **Acorn Topper**, *above*, for any package. Instructions are on page 102.

Knit a **Soft Baby Mobile**, *above right*, in shapes that any little one would love to watch. Sun, stars, moons, and clouds are knit and then lightly stuffed before hanging. Wrap the gift in a **Simple Star Wrap**, *above left*, that reflects the sweet gift.

Create a **Stamped Baby Picture Frame**, *opposite*, using a rubber stamp and ink pad. Choose colors that match the treasured photo in the frame. Instructions are on pages 102–103.

Dressed-Up Tree Wrap

Shown on page 86

WHAT YOU NEED

Gift box
White wrapping paper
Large tree cookie cutter
Small star cookie cutter
Crafts glue
Various sizes of green ready-made
  bows
1 gold ready-made bow
Decorative ribbon (optional)

WHAT YOU DO

Wrap gift in white wrapping paper. Place crafts glue around the entire edge of the tree cookie cutter and glue it to center of package. Glue around the entire edge of the star cookie cutter and place at the top of the tree on package. Put the various sizes of green bows into the Christmas tree cookie cutter in a manner that is pleasing to the eye. You may need to remove the backing of some bows to make them stick to the package. They should stay in place if they are stuffed in rather tightly. Layer bows upon bows for a fuller effect. Place the gold bow in the star cookie cutter. Add decorative ribbon if desired.

Embellished Knitted Mittens

Shown on page 87

SKILL LEVEL: Intermediate
SIZES: Girls' size 4 (6, 8).
FINISHED MEASUREMENTS:
Width: 3 (3¼, 3½)"
Length: 6½ (7, 7½)"

WHAT YOU NEED

Lion Brand, Wool-Ease Chunky, Article
  #630, 80% acrylic/ 20% wool yarn
  (153 yards per ball): One ball of #140
  Deep Rose
Size 6 (4mm) knitting needles or size
  needed to obtain gauge
Size 4 (3.5mm) knitting needles
Yarn needle
Two ring-type stitch markers
Assorted scraps wool or wool felt
Assorted colors embroidery floss
Tracing paper, marking pen
Large-eye sewing needle

GAUGE: In St st with larger needles (knit RS rows, purl WS rows), 16 sts and 23 rows = 4"/10 cm. TAKE TIME TO CHECK YOUR GAUGE.

SPECIAL ABBREVIATIONS:

M1: Lift running thread before next stitch onto left-hand needle and knit in its back loop to make one stitch.
Ssk: Slip next 2 sts knitwise, one at a time to right-hand needle, insert tip of left-hand needle into fronts of these 2 sts and ktog.
Pm: Place a marker.

WHAT YOU DO

MITTEN (Make two alike)
CUFF: With smaller needles, cast on 25 (27, 29) sts.

RIBBING

Row 1 (WS): (P1, k1) across, ending p1.
Row 2: (K1, p1) across, ending k1.
Rep rows 1-2 until cuff measures 2 (2½, 2½)", ending WS. Beg with a knit row work 2 (4, 4) rows St st.

THUMB

Row 1 (RS): K12 (13, 14), pm, M1, k1, M1, k to end of row.
Row 2: Purl across.
Row 3: K to marker, sl marker, M1, k to marker, M1, k to end of row.
Rep rows 2-3 until there are 9 (11, 11) sts bet markers. P 1 row.
Next Row: K across, removing markers and placing thumb sts onto a spare strand of yarn. Cont St st on the 24 (26, 28) sts until piece measures approx 5½ (6, 6½)" from beg, ending with a WS row and placing a marker after the 12th (13th, 14th) st.

TOP SHAPING

Row 1 (RS): Ssk, k to 2 sts before marker, k2tog, sl marker, ssk, k to last 2 sts, k2tog.
Row 2: Purl across.
Rep last 2 rows until 16 (18, 20) sts rem. (K2tog) across – 8 (9, 10) sts. Leaving a long tail, cut yarn.

CLOSURE

Thread tail into yarn needle. Beg with the last st on needle, take yarn back through rem sts, twice. Pull up to tightly close opening. Leave tail for joining sides.

embroidery floss, stitch shapes onto mittens using decorative embroidery stitches (buttonhole stitch, running stitch, French knots, lazy daisy stitches). If added dimension is desired, stitch buttonhole stitch around shape first and then tack onto background shape by stitching in center of second shape only, keeping edges free.

Beaded Silver Necklace
Shown on page 88

THUMB
With the RS facing, return sts to larger needle. Join yarn and k9 (11, 11).
Next Row: P3 (4, 4), p2tog, p4 (5, 5). Work 2 (4, 4) more St st rows on the 8 (10, 10) sts. (K2tog) across. Rep Closure as for Top Shaping. Join thumb seam. Darn opening closed. Weave in loose ends.

EMBELLISHING
Trace desired patterns, *below,* onto tracing paper. Cut shapes out of wool or wool felt. Layer shapes onto center of knitted mittens. Using three strands

WHAT YOU NEED
12×12-inch piece of felt or beading dish
2 crimp beads
One large ⅝-inch bead in blue and yellow
2 cylindrical ⅜-inch beads in clear and blue tones
4 silver rhinestone beads
8 1-inch-long silver beads
4 round blue beads
2 opaque ⅜-inch blue beads
14 aqua blue seed beads
40 elongated aqua blue beads
Desired silver necklace closure

Crimping tool
22-inch piece of beading wire
Beading wire cutters

WHAT YOU DO
1. Lay beads in the beading dish or on the felt in the order to be strung. Using the crimping tool, crimp beads, beading wire, and closure, attach the beading wire to one end of the closure, looping it through the opening and back through about ½ inch. Slide a crimp bead over both strands of wire and use the crimping tool to secure by squeezing the crimp bead.
2. Thread the beads onto the wire in the following order: 5 seed beads, 5 elongated blue beads, 1 rhinestone circle bead, 3 elongated blue beads, 1 round bead, 3 elongated blue beads, 1 long silver bead, 3 elongated blue beads, 1 cylindrical ⅜-inch bead, 3 elongated blue beads, 1 long silver bead, 1 seed bead, 1 blue ball bead, 1 seed bead, 1 long silver bead, 3 elongated blue beads, 1 rhinestone bead, and the center bead.

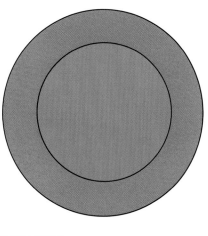

EMBELLISHED KNITTED MITTENS
Full-Size Patterns

3. Reverse this order to complete other side of the necklace, ending with a crimp bead. When beading is complete, slide the wire through the other side of the closure opening, crimp bead, and tuck the end through the beaded beads. Crimp to secure and trim excess beading wire.

Paper Rose Topper
Shown on page 88

WHAT YOU NEED
12-inch sheet of red or raspberry color lightweight cardstock
Scrap of green lightweight cardstock
Green and purple watercolor paints
Water
2 custard cups or small dishes
Crafts glue

WHAT YOU DO
1. Tear the red paper into four round pieces: Tear one about 3½ inches, one about 2½×2 inches, and one 1×2 inches. Tear one piece in the shape of an L, 1½ inches across at the bottom by 2½-inches tall. Tear the green paper into a 1×2½-inch piece to resemble a leaf.
2. In one custard cup mix water with the purple watercolor to make a dark color. In the other cup mix water with green watercolor to make a dark color.
3. Dip the edges of each of the pieces into the water, letting the colored water bleed into the torn edges of the paper. Allow to dry.

4. Layer and glue the large piece on the bottom, then the center piece, then the smaller piece. Curl the L-shape piece and glue for a rose center. Glue the leaf under the rose piece.

Holiday Surprise Holders
Shown on page 89

WHAT YOU NEED FOR EACH BOX
Tracing paper; pencil
8×8-inch piece of lightweight printed cardstock
Scissors; ruler
Scoring tool; paper punch
Crafts glue
10-inch length of narrow ribbon
Sticker in desired design

WHAT YOU DO
Enlarge and trace the desired pattern, *below* and *opposite*. Cut out. Trace the fold lines on the wrong side of the pattern. Lay the ruler on the fold line and use a scoring tool or open scissors to score on the line. Use a paper punch to make a hole for the ribbon. Fold along the lines and glue together. Tie a knot in the ribbon and thread through the hole,

leaving the knot on the outside. Thread the other side of the ribbon through the other hole and make a knot on the outside to secure. Place a sticker on the front of the box.

Gifty Purse Card
Shown on page 89

WHAT YOU NEED
Tracing paper
Pencil
Scissors

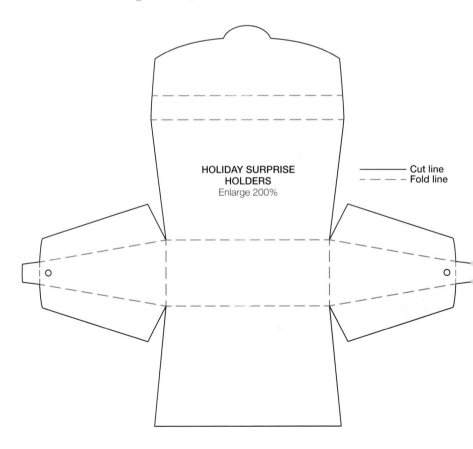

HOLIDAY SURPRISE
HOLDERS
Enlarge 200%

—— Cut line
- - - Fold line

Purchased card blank (available at crafts stores)
8×8-inch piece of cardstock
2 clothespins; waxed paper
Crafts glue
Fine gold glitter
6-inch piece of gold cording or ribbon
Gold alphabet stickers
Gold jewel

WHAT YOU DO

1. Trace the full-size pattern, *right*. Cut purse body shape from cardstock. Score and fold along fold lines.

2. Glue the sides of the purse body together just along the edges, leaving the top open. Use clothespins to hold the purse together while it is drying. Set aside to dry. Fold flap down over purse body.

3. Remove clothespins from the purse and lay the paper purse on waxed paper. Use the crafts glue to make a thin line of glue around the flap edge and the sides of the purse. Dust with glitter. Allow to dry.

4. Glue the purse to the card blank front. Tuck and glue the cording or ribbon behind the purse for a handle. Glue the jewel to the front flap. Allow to dry. Fold and tuck money into the purse. Write a message on the card using the alphabet stickers.

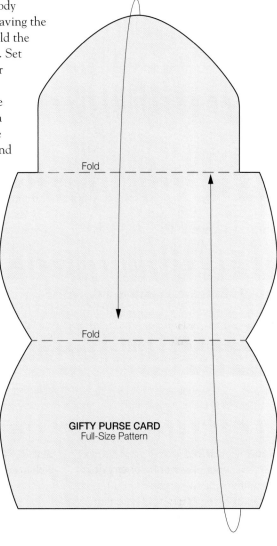

Fold

Fold

GIFTY PURSE CARD
Full-Size Pattern

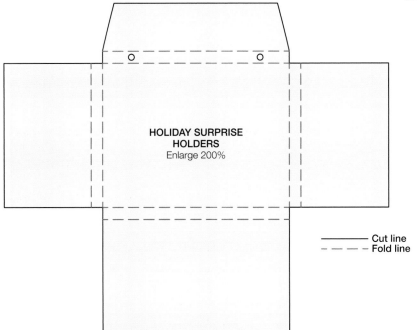

HOLIDAY SURPRISE
HOLDERS
Enlarge 200%

——— Cut line
– – – Fold line

Pattern Wrap
Shown on page 90

WHAT YOU NEED
Pattern tissue from dress pattern
Scissors; transparent tape
Box to be wrapped
Scraps of rickrack
Buttons
Crafts glue
Printed scrapbook paper; string (optional)

WHAT YOU DO
Lay out multiple pieces (about three) of pattern tissue and, treating the pieces as one, cut a piece large enough to wrap the box. Wrap and secure with tape. Glue rickrack and buttons to decorate. Add a tag if desired.

Tissue Bow
Shown on page 90

WHAT YOU NEED
Pattern tissue from dress pattern
Scissors
Paper clip
Small Christmas ornament (optional)
Crafts glue
Narrow ribbon

WHAT YOU DO
Lay multiple layers (about 4 layers) of pattern tissue together. Cut a 7×11-inch rectangle, cutting through all of the layers. Treating the layers as one piece, accordion-fold tissue, making 1½-inch folds. Place the paper clip in the center of the folded tissue. Open and pull apart the tissue on both sides, fluffing tissue until it looks like a bow. Glue a small ornament to the center of the bow if desired. Slide the ribbon through the back of the paper clip and tie to the package.

Printed Fabric Wraps
Shown on page 90

WHAT YOU NEED
Round gift box
Printed fabric big enough
   to wrap gift
Transparent tape
Scissors
Ribbon

WHAT YOU DO
Measure fabric around gift box, leaving enough extra fabric to extend on each side. Place fabric around gift box and tape

where fabric meets. Gather the fabric at one end and tie tightly with ribbon; repeat at the opposite end.

Candy Stripe Jar
Shown on page 91

WHAT YOU NEED
Clear glass jar with lid
Glass paints
1-inch foam brush
Small paintbrush

WHAT YOU DO
Wash and dry jar and avoid touching areas to be painted. Following manufacturer's directions, paint the jar. Use the foam brush to paint wide stripes at an angle on the sides of the jar. Paint small red and white checks around the top of the jar. Add dots of green at the top of the wide lines. Paint the jar lid top red. Let dry. Paint green dots on the rest of the lid. Add white dots on the dry red paint.

Monogrammed Handkerchieves
Shown on page 91

WHAT YOU NEED
Purchased white or striped
   handkerchief
Transfer paper
Embroidery needle and hoop
Embroidery floss in
   desired colors

WHAT YOU DO
Wash and press handkerchief. Trace desired letter or motif on the corner of handkerchief using transfer paper. With embroidery floss, use stem stitch to embroider letter. Use French knots and stem stitch around letter. For embroidery stitch diagrams and instructions, see *page 159.*

MONOGRAMMED HANDKERCHIEVES
Decorative Motifs
Embroidery Patterns

**MONOGRAMMED
HANDKERCHIEVES
Alphabet**
Embroidery Patterns

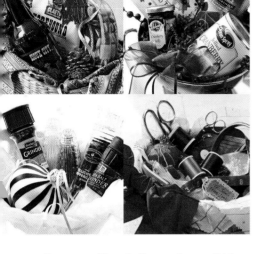

Personalized Container Gifts
Shown on page 92

For the Old-Fashioned Basket: Use a medium-size basket with open top. Cut the fabric large enough to fit into the basket and drape over the sides. Fill the basket with sarsparilla, horehound drops, and Christmas candies. Tie a vintage cookie cutter to the sack of candy. Add some fresh greenery, gift tag, and pinecone.

For the Cranberry Goodie Basket: Use a red colander. Fill the container with cranberry products, such as cranberry jelly, cranberry iced tea, and canned cranberries. Add red shred around the items. Tuck in berry sprigs, a red bow, and a gift tag.

For the Basket in Black and White: Line a clear bowl with a starched white napkin or white tissue. Fill with a variety of seasoned salts, sea salt, peppercorns, and a pepper grinder. Add a black-and-white ornament and a tag.

For the Sewing Basket: Use a medium-size basket. Use pinking shears to cut pieces of pattern tissue to line the basket. Fill with shears, trim scissors, embroidery hoop, spools of red and green thread, a red tape measure, and pins. Add a gift tag and a red bow.

Acorn Toppers
Shown on page 93

WHAT YOU NEED
Acorn tops (see Sources, *page 159*)
Small gold jingle bells to fit inside tops
Crafts glue; narrow gold ribbon

WHAT YOU DO
Note: Because acorn tops are from nature, they can vary in size. Small jingle bells come in a variety of sizes. Purchase bells to fit the tops.

Be sure the tops are clean and dry. Glue the bell inside the top. Allow to dry. Wrap the gift with narrow gold ribbon. Group the bell-filled tops on the ribbon. Allow to dry.

Simple Star Wrap
Shown on page 94

WHAT YOU NEED
Tracing paper; pencil
Scissors
Cardstock in blue and pink
Gift to wrap
White print wrapping paper
White alphabet stickers
Wide sheer ribbon
Paper punch
Pink and blue narrow ribbons

1. Trace the star pattern, *below.* Trace around the pattern onto blue and pink cardstock and cut out. Cut three stars. Put baby's name on one star. Set aside.
2. Wrap the package and tie the wide sheer ribbon around the box. Punch holes in the stars and thread the ribbons through the holes. Tie on the package.

Soft Baby Mobile
Shown on page 94

SKILL LEVEL: Intermediate
FINISHED MEASUREMENTS:
5" diameter for Cloud and Star
6½" diameter for Sun
5" length for Moon

WHAT YOU NEED
Cottontots from Bernat (Art. 164090)
100% cotton; 3½ oz. (100 g);
171 yds. (156 m); worsted weight

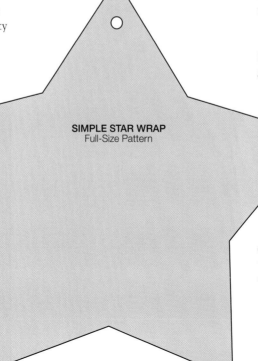

SIMPLE STAR WRAP
Full-Size Pattern

1 ball #90230 Sweet Green (A)
1 ball #90129 Blue Berry (B)
1 ball #90421 Strawberry (C)
1 ball #90615 Sunshine (D)
1 ball #90016 Lemon Berry (E)
1 ball #90005 Wonder White (F)
Size H/8 (5 mm) crochet hook OR SIZE
    NEEDED TO OBTAIN GAUGE
Polyester fiberfill
4½ yards of ½"-wide ribbon
Blunt-end yarn needle

GAUGE: 14 sc and 14 rows = 4" (10 cm).
TAKE TIME TO CHECK YOUR
GAUGE.

WHAT YOU DO
STAR (make 2 each with A, B, and C)
Ch 2.
Rnd 1: Work 5 sc in 2nd ch from hook.
Place marker to mark beg of rnd.
Rnd 2: Work (sc, ch 1, sc) in each st around.
Rnd 3: *Sk 1 sc, (2 sc, ch 2, 2 sc) in next
ch-1 sp, sk 1 sc; rep from * around.
Rnd 4: *Sk sc, sc in next sc; in next ch-2
sp work 2 sc, ch 2, and 2 sc; sc in next sc;
sk sc; rep from * around.
Rnd 5: *Sk sc, sc in each of next 2 sc,
(2 sc, ch 2, 2 sc) in next ch-2 sp, sc in
each of next 2 sc, sk sc; rep from *
around, join with sl st to first sc; fasten
off. Make 2nd side to match, but do not
fasten off. Place WS of first side against
WS of 2nd side, lining up sts.
Joining rnd: Working through both
thicknesses, *sk sc, sc in each of next
3 sc; 2 sc, ch 2, 2 sc in next ch-2 sp; sc
each of next 3 sc, sk sc; rep from * around,
stuff with fiberfill before completing rnd;
join with sl st to first sc; fasten off.

CLOUD (make 2)
With F, ch 6.
Rnd 1: Work 3 sc in 2nd ch from hook,
sc in each of next 3 ch, 3 sc in last ch,
working along opposite side of foundation
ch, work sc in each of rem 3 ch—12 sc.
Place marker to mark beg of rnd.
Rnd 2: *Work 2 sc in each of next 3 sts,
sc in each of next 3 sts; rep from * once
more—18 sc.
Rnd 3: *Work (2 sc in next st, sc in next
st) 3 times, sc in each of next 3 sts; rep
from * once more—24 sc.
Rnd 4: *Work (2 sc in next st, sc in each
of next 2 sts) 3 times, sc in each of next
3 sts; rep from * once more—30 sc.
Rnd 5: *Sk 2 sts, 8 dc in next st, sk 2 sts,
sl st in next st; rep from * 4 more times;
fasten off.
Make 2nd side to match, but do not
fasten off. Place WS of first side against
WS of 2nd side, lining up sts and join
pieces tog with a rnd of sc; stuff with
fiberfill before completing rnd; join with
sl st to first sc; fasten off.

MOON (make 2)
With D, ch 2.
Row 1: Work 3 sc in 2nd ch from hook;
turn.
Row 2: Ch 1, 2 sc in first sc, 3 sc in next
sc, 2 sc in last sc; turn.
Row 3: Ch 3—counts as dc; dc in first sc,
2 hdc in next sc, 2 sc in each of next 3 sc,
2 hdc in next sc, 2 dc in last sc; turn.
Row 4: Ch 3—counts as dc; dc in first st,
hdc in next st, (2 sc in next st, sc in each
of next 2 sts) 3 times, 2 sc in next st, hdc
in next st, 2 dc in last st; turn.
Row 5: Ch 3—counts as dc; dc in first st,
hdc in next st, (2 sc in next st, sc in each
of next 4 sts) 3 times, 2 sc in next st, hdc
in next st, 2 dc in last st; turn.
Row 6: Ch 3—counts as dc; 2 dc in first
st, hdc in next st, (2 sc in next st, sc in
each of next 2 sts) 7 times, 2 sc in next st,
hdc in next st, 3 dc in last st; fasten off.
Make 2nd side to match, but do not
fasten off. Place WS of first side against
WS of 2nd side, lining up sts and join
pieces tog with a rnd of sc, working
(2 sc, ch 2, 2 sc) in each point; stuff with
fiberfill before completing rnd; join with
sl st to first sc; fasten off.

SUN
Center (make 2)
With E, ch 2.
Rnd 1: Work 7 sc in 2nd ch from hook;
place marker to mark beg of rnd.
Rnds 2 and 4: Work 2 sc in each st
around—28 sc after Rnd 4 is completed.
Rnds 3 and 5: Sc in each st around.
Rnd 6: *Work 2 sc in next st, sc in next
st; rep from * around—42 sts; fasten off.
Make 2nd center to match, but do not
fasten off. Place WS of first center against
WS of 2nd center, lining up sts.
Rnd 7: Join with a rnd of sc, stuff with
fiberfill before completing rnd—42 sc.

Sun Rays
Rnd 8: *Sk 2 sts, (3 dc, ch 1, tr, ch 1,
3 dc) in next st, sk 2 sts, sl st in next st,
rep from * 6 more times; fasten off.

FINISHING
Weave in all ends. Attach assorted
lengths of ribbon to each motif.

Stamped Baby Picture Frame
Shown on page 95

WHAT YOU NEED
White wood picture frame
Snowflake-motif rubber stamps in a
    variety of sizes
Blue and purple stamp pads suitable
    for stamping on wood
3-dimensional white snowflake sticker

WHAT YOU DO
Be sure the frame is clean and dry. Use
the stamps to randomly stamp blue and
purple snowflakes on the frame edge.
Let dry. Add the sticker.

There's no place like home for the holidays—
so make it special with your own personal touch.

christmas at
home

Show that you care by placing a candle in the window. Make clever

Paper-Covered Candles, *opposite*, using battery candles and mini-print

scrapbook papers. Greet guests to your holiday home with a traditional

Holiday Door Welcome, *above*. Surround the door with greenery, then add

a festive white stocking, a hint that Christmas is near. Instructions, page 112.

A Fraser fir is decorated with dried artichokes, pear gourds, and dyed eucalyptus for a colorful **Coming Home Tree**, *opposite*. Soft winter suede and cool metallic fabrics combine to create elegant **Shadow-Quilted Snowflake Pillows**, *above*. The patterns on the pillows each reflect a different snowflake shape. Instructions for these projects begin on page 112.

Weave beautiful holiday ribbons together to make stunning Woven
Ribbon Pillows, *below*. The ribbons are woven, then treated as one piece
of fabric to make the pillows. Instructions are on pages 114.

Beaded Holiday Coasters, *above*, make it easy to cozy up at home with warm or chilled drinks. Christmas fabric is wrapped around a plastic canvas to create each coaster. Instructions are on pages 114–115.

Swirls of white cording cover bright-color cardboard circles for a sweet **Lollipop Welcome**, *right*. The faux candy treats are surrounded by greenery in a sturdy outdoor planter.

Light the way with easy-to-make **Pretty Paper Luminarias**, *above*. Use a cookie cutter shape to make the pattern on the front or use one of the patterns given. Instructions and patterns for all these projects are on pages 115–116.

A cast-off sweater is felted, sewn into oversize mittens, and then filled with greenery and red berries. This cozy pair is then attached to a fresh green wreath to make a **Winter Mitten Wreath**, *above*. Instructions are on page 117.

christmas at home

Holiday Door Welcome

Shown on page 104

WHAT YOU NEED

Garlands of fresh greenery
Pinecones
24 gauge wire
Bow in desired color
Purchased white stocking
White tissue paper
Greenery and berry picks

WHAT YOU DO

Lay out the greenery and wire in pinecones about every 10 inches. Tack around the top of the door. Attach the bow to the front of the door. If using a long stocking, cut off and turn over cuff. Fill the stocking with white tissue paper. Add greenery and berries in the top of the stocking. Attach to bow on the door.

Paper-Covered Candles

Shown on page 105

WHAT YOU NEED

Purchased battery candles
4×3-inch piece of printed scrapbook paper
1×3-inch piece of plain-color scrapbook paper
Crafts glue
Rubberbands

WHAT YOU DO

1. Most battery-operated candles are a standard size; however, measure around the candle to be sure the paper fits before cutting. Wrap the candle around the candle stem. Run a line of glue along the edge of the paper to adhere the two ends together. See Photo A.

2. Place rubberbands around the paper to hold until dry. See Photo B. Repeat with the other small piece of paper at the base of the candle. Allow to dry. Remove the rubberbands.

Coming Home Tree

Shown on page 106

WHAT YOU NEED

Potted or cut Fraser fir tree
Large pot to fit tree
Purchased pinecone garland (available at crafts stores)
24 gauge wire
Wire cutters
Dried artichokes
Pear gourds
Dried eucalyptus
Dried or fresh caspia
Astilbe seedpods
Dried hydrangea blooms

WHAT YOU DO

Place tree in pot. If using a cut tree, surround the tree with fresh soil to secure. Place pinecone garland on tree, tucking it into the branches. If necessary, wire the items, such as the pear gourds, to place on the tree. Many of the items, such as the dried artichokes, can be tucked into the tree without wiring. Continue adding items until tree is very full and desired effect is achieved.

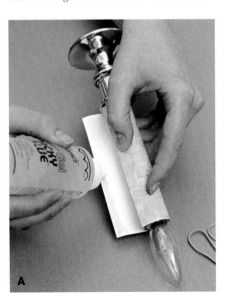

A

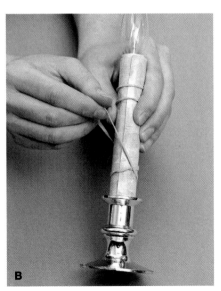

B

Shadow-Quilted Snowflake Pillows
Shown on page 107

WHAT YOU NEED
Tracing paper; marking pen
For the light blue pillow:
⅓ yard light blue suede-like fabric
    (nonraveling), cut into two 13-inch
    squares
One 13-inch square of dark blue
    metallic fabric
1½ yards of ⅜-inch-wide cording
12-inch square pillow form
Matching light blue thread
For the dark blue pillow:
½ yard medium-blue suede-like fabric
    (nonraveling), cut into two 15-inch
    squares
One 15-inch square silver metallic fabric
1¾ yards silver beaded trim
14-inch square pillow form
Matching medium-blue thread

WHAT YOU DO
1. Enlarge and trace patterns, *right*. For
pillow front, place right side of metallic
fabric to wrong side of blue fabrics. Baste
¼ inch around outside edges. Center
snowflake pattern to center back of
metallic fabric. Pin in place. Working
from the wrong side of the pillow front,
machine-stitch around lines of design
using matching sewing thread. Turn over;
on the front side, carefully clip away only
the blue fabric inside the stitching lines
to reveal metallic fabric underneath.
Remove paper from the back of the
pillow top.
2. Baste cording or trim around pillow
front. Place pillow backing right sides
together with the top. Stitch around
outside edges using a ½-inch seam,
leaving opening to insert pillow form.
Clip corners and turn right side out.
Insert pillow form. Using matching
thread, slip-stitch opening closed.

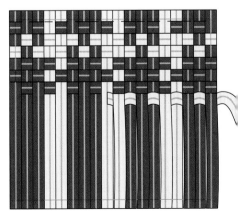

Woven Ribbon Pillows

Shown on page 108

WHAT YOU NEED

For square pillow:
One 14×14-inch pillow form
14 yards of 1-inch-wide ribbon in
    desired color and pattern
Two 15×15-inch pieces of fabric

For rectangular pillow:
One 14×16-inch pillow form
15 yards 1-inch-wide ribbon
Two 15×17-inch pieces fabric

WHAT YOU DO

1. Cut ribbon into 16 lengths, 1½ inches longer than the fabric dimension length. See Step 1, *below.* Plan desired color pattern to cover total pillow top or refer to pattern illustrations, *below.* Beginning at one end, hand- or machine-baste one edge of each lengthwise ribbon to edge of fabric top, extending edge of ribbon about ½ inch beyond fabric. See Step 2, *below.*
2. Begin weaving ribbon using crosswise strips, laying ribbon edges close to each adjoining length. See Step 3, *below.* Pin through ribbon and fabric at ends.
3. When weaving is complete, baste around outside edges about ¼ inch from edge of ribbon and fabric through ribbon ends and fabric top.
4. With right sides together, carefully stitch the pillow top to fabric backing, leaving a 6-inch opening to insert pillow form. Turn right side out. Insert pillow form. Handstitch opening closed.

Beaded Holiday Coasters

Shown on page 109

WHAT YOU NEED

⅛ yard Christmas print fabric
Scraps cotton batting
1 sheet plastic canvas
Assorted glass beads
Glass seed beads
Matching thread

WHAT YOU DO

1. Cut fabric into four 4½×8½-inch pieces. Cut batting into four 4×8-inch pieces. Cut plastic canvas into four 3⅞-inch squares.

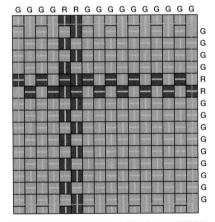

SQUARE WOVEN RIBBON PILLOW PATTERN

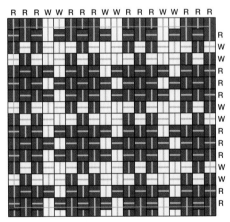

RECTANGLE WOVEN RIBBON PILLOW PATTERN

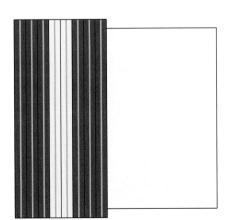

Step 1

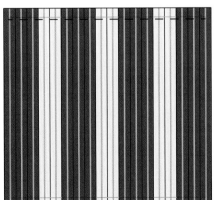

Step 2

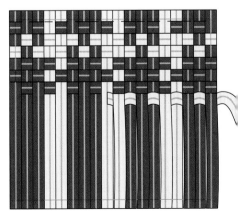

Step 3

2. Wrap batting around plastic canvas square. Stitch batting around canvas by whip-stitching over canvas edges. With right sides together, fold print fabric in half to make squares. Stitch sides using ¼-inch seam allowance and leaving one end open. Turn right side out. Insert batting-wrapped plastic canvas squares. Sew open edge closed with small stitches using matching sewing thread.

3. Using a double sewing thread, sew a few securing stitches at one corner of the coaster square. Thread needle through beads, looping over smallest seed bead at the end and back through beads to the corner edge of the coaster square. Pull thread tight, sew a couple of securing stitches in the corner of the fabric, and tie off thread length by burying the knot in the layers of batting inside the coaster. Continue threading beads and securing to each corner of the coaster.

PRETTY PAPER LUMINARIAS
Full-Size Patterns

Pretty Paper Luminarias
Shown on page 110

WHAT YOU NEED
Tracing paper
Paper sacks in red and gold, large
    enough to hold a canning jar or
    glass tumbler
Heavy cardboard or wood
    to fit in sack

Lollipop Welcome
Shown on page 110

WHAT YOU NEED
FOR 3 LOLLIPOPS

Three ¼×30-inch dowels
White acrylic paint
Paintbrush
Three 9-inch cardboard cake rounds
Red and green printed cardstock
Spray-fix glue
3 yards ½-inch-wide white cording
Pencil; crafts glue
Scissors
Strapping or duct tape
Large planter
Fresh greenery or tree toppers
Berry picks
Bow (optional)

Crafts knife
Glitter glue
Canning jar or glass tumbler
Green crafting sand
Green votive candle

WHAT YOU DO

1. Trace the patterns, *page 115*, and cut out. Transfer pattern to front of sack. Place heavy cardboard or wood inside sack to prevent cutting through to the other side. Cut out pattern using crafts knife. Outline design with glitter glue. Allow to dry.

2. Fill the jar or tumbler half full with green crafting sand. See Photo, *above*. Center votive candle in the sands. Light candle.

Never leave a burning candle unattended.

A

B

C

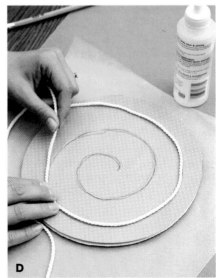

D

WHAT YOU DO

1. Paint dowels using white acrylic paint. Allow to dry. Set aside.

2. Trace around the cardboard cake rounds onto the cardstock. See Photo A. Cut out. Spray the round and glue the cardstock to the cardboard. Allow to dry. Use a pencil to draw a swirl on the cardboard. See Photo B. Make a line of glue along the pencil line and glue the cording to the cardstock using crafts glue. See Photos C and D. Allow to dry.

3. Tape the dowel to the back of the circle.

4. Fill the planter with fresh greenery or tree toppers. Insert berry picks. Poke the paper lollipops into the greenery. Add a bow if desired.

Winter Mitten Wreath

Shown on page 111

WHAT YOU NEED

Four 8×11-inch pieces of felted wool
    patterned sweater
Tracing paper; pencil
Matching sewing thread
12-inch piece of coordinating yarn
Large needle
24-inch fresh green wreath
2-inch-wide ribbon for bow
Floral wire; tissue paper
Sprigs of red berries

WHAT YOU DO

1. *Note:* For tips on felting sweaters, *see page 159.* Enlarge and trace pattern, *right,* and cut out. Lay pattern onto felted sweater pieces, placing flat opening end of mitten at finished ribbing edges of sweater. Cut four mitten shapes from fabric, reversing two to make mirror images. With right sides together, sew around side and lower curved edges, using a ¼-inch seam, leaving mitten opening unstitched. Clip curves and turn right side out. Press. Thread needle with yarn. Tie a knot in one end and pull through at sides to connect mittens.

2. Make a bow and wire to top of wreath. Stuff mittens slightly with tissue paper. Attach mittens to wreath at bow. Place berry sprigs in tops of mittens.

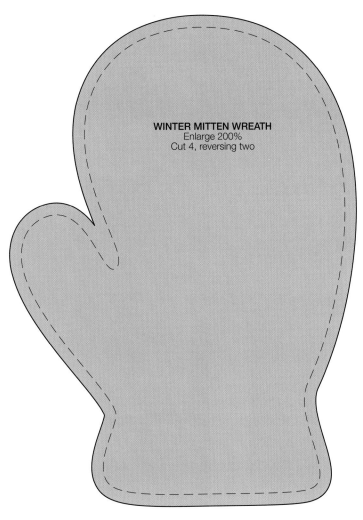

WINTER MITTEN WREATH
Enlarge 200%
Cut 4, reversing two

During this festive season, buffet-style soup suppers are one delicious way to serve guests. Choose from three simple soups, breads, salads, and desserts.

hearty
soup suppers

Warm up to richly spiced **Fireside Chili**, *opposite*. It's sure to

become a favorite for winter gatherings. Accompany the chili

with savory **Pepper-Cornmeal Biscuits**, *above*, spread with

Chipotle Butter. Recipes are on page 125.

Fresh salads with invigorating flavors pair perfectly with hearty soups. **Butterhead Salad with Smoky Ranch Dressing,** *right,* comes with lively homemade dressing. **Fresh Citrus and Cranberry Salad,** *right,* has a refreshing burst of mint and ginger. Recipes are on page 126.

Mexican spices infuse **Sweet Potato and Hominy Stew**, *above*. Wholesome **Soup Sticks** and **Spicy Honey-Butter**, *left*, are crisp, warm serve-alongs. Recipes are on pages 126–127.

Jazz up baguette slices with butter and herbs to make **Garlic-Herbed Bread**, which goes well with any soup or salad. Recipe is on page 127.

Add bold flavor to **Spinach Salad with Brie Toast**, *above,* with cranberry dressing. The elegant pureed **Butternut Squash Bisque**, *left,* is a welcome warmer. Recipes are on pages 127–128.

Indulge in dessert! Seasonal flavors—peppermint, pumpkin, chocolate, citrus, and cranberries—star in this lineup. Try **Peppermint-Fudge Pie,** *above left,* **Pumpkin-Pecan Tassies,** *above right,* and **Chocolate Loaf with Winter Fruit Glaze,** *right.* Recipes are on pages 128–129.

Pepper-Cornmeal Biscuits

Make this confetti bread about 30 minutes before serving begins so it's nice and warm.

Shown on page 118

WHAT YOU NEED

2 cups all-purpose flour
1 cup yellow cornmeal
2 tablespoons sugar
1½ teaspoons baking powder
½ teaspoon salt
½ cup cold butter, cubed
1 cup buttermilk
¼ cup chopped roasted red pepper
1 jalapeño pepper, seeded and finely chopped*
  Buttermilk
  Paprika
  Chipotle Butter

WHAT YOU DO

1. Preheat oven to 425°F. In a large bowl stir together flour, cornmeal, sugar, baking powder, and salt.
2. Add butter to flour mixture; cut into flour mixture with pastry blender until it resembles coarse crumbs. Make a well in the center of the flour-butter mixture. Add 1 cup buttermilk and chopped peppers; stir with spoon until moistened. Do not overmix. (If dough appears dry, add 1 to 2 tablespoons additional buttermilk.)
3. Turn dough out onto floured surface. Gently knead by lifting and folding dough, 4 or 5 times, giving a quarter turn after each knead. Roll into 8-inch square, ¾ inch thick. Cut into 2-inch squares. Place squares 1 inch apart on ungreased baking sheet. Brush with buttermilk;

sprinkle with paprika. Bake for 12 to 15 minutes or until lightly browned. Serve warm with Chipotle Butter. Makes 16 biscuits.
Chipotle Butter: Combine ½ cup butter, softened, and 1 canned chipotle pepper in adobo sauce, chopped.
*Test Kitchen Tip: Because chile peppers contain volatile oils that can burn your skin and eyes, avoid direct contact with them as much as possible. When working with chile peppers, wear plastic or rubber gloves. If your bare hands do touch the peppers, wash your hands and nails well with soap and warm water.

Fireside Chili

The bit of bittersweet chocolate in this chili is optional, but try it—it keeps the heat of the chili seasoning in check and adds richness.

Shown on page 119

WHAT YOU NEED

  Chili Seasoning Puree
1½ pounds ground beef chuck
1 large onion, chopped
2 stalks celery, sliced
2 tablespoons smoked paprika
2 teaspoons ground coriander
1 teaspoon crushed red pepper
¼ to ½ teaspoon ground cloves
1 28-ounce can whole tomatoes, cut up
1½ cups water
1 14-ounce can beef broth
1 6-ounce can tomato paste
1 to 2 ounces bittersweet chocolate, chopped (optional)

1½ cups dried plums (prunes) or raisins, chopped
  Sour cream and snipped chives (optional)

WHAT YOU DO

1. Prepare Chili Seasoning Puree. In a 6-quart Dutch oven cook beef, onion, and celery until meat is browned, stirring as needed. Drain off fat.
2. Stir in Chili Seasoning Puree, paprika, coriander, crushed red pepper, and cloves. Cook and stir for 2 minutes. Stir in undrained tomatoes, the water, beef broth, and tomato paste. Bring to boiling; reduce heat. Add chocolate, if desired, and plums. Simmer, covered, for 1 hour, stirring occasionally. Serve topped with sour cream and chives. Makes 8 servings.
Chili Seasoning Puree: Place 2 dried ancho, mulato, or pasilla chile peppers in a small bowl. Add enough boiling water to cover. Let stand for 30 minutes. Drain well; remove stems and seeds.* In a food processor or blender combine the drained chile peppers; ¾ cup beef broth; 1 fresh jalapeño pepper, seeded and chopped;* and 5 pitted dried plums. Cover and process or blend until smooth.
*Test Kitchen Tip: Because chile peppers contain volatile oils that can burn your skin and eyes, avoid direct contact with them as much as possible. When working with chile peppers, wear plastic or rubber gloves. If your bare hands do touch the peppers, wash your hands and nails well with soap and water.

Butterhead Salad with Smoky Ranch Dressing

Shown on page 120

WHAT YOU NEED

- 1 clove garlic, peeled
- ½ teaspoon salt
- 1 cup buttermilk
- ⅓ cup mayonnaise
- ⅓ cup sour cream
- 2 tablespoons snipped fresh Italian parsley
- 2 tablespoons snipped fresh chives
- 2 tablespoons thinly sliced green onion (1)
- 1 teaspoon white wine vinegar
- ½ teaspoon smoked paprika
- ¼ teaspoon black pepper
- 4 heads butterhead (Boston or Bibb) lettuce, torn
- 1 cup yellow pear tomatoes and/or red cherry tomatoes, halved

WHAT YOU DO

1. For dressing, place garlic clove on a cutting board. Using the side of a wide knife, smash garlic. Sprinkle with salt; mash and rub garlic into a paste with side of knife. Transfer to a medium bowl. Whisk in buttermilk, mayonnaise, sour cream, parsley, chives, green onion, vinegar, paprika, and pepper until combined.

2. On individual serving plates arrange lettuce with tomatoes. Drizzle with dressing. Makes 8 servings.

To Make Ahead: Prepare dressing as directed. Transfer to an airtight container; cover. Store in the refrigerator up to 1 week.

Fresh Citrus and Cranberry Salad

The cranberry topper is also a crunchy, good-for-you accompaniment to sliced turkey. Shown on page 120

WHAT YOU NEED

- 2 cups fresh or frozen cranberries, thawed
- 4 oranges
- 1 cup thinly sliced celery (2 stalks)
- ⅓ cup finely chopped onion
- ¼ cup sugar
- 2 tablespoons fresh lemon juice
- 1 teaspoon grated fresh ginger
- 1 5-ounce package baby arugula
- ¼ cup fresh mint leaves, chopped
- 2 tablespoons walnut oil or olive oil

WHAT YOU DO

1. For cranberry topper, in food processor cover and pulse cranberries 5 times to coarsely chop (or coarsely chop by hand). Transfer to a bowl.

2. Cut peel from oranges. Section oranges over bowl to catch juice. Add sections and juice to cranberries. Stir in celery, onion, sugar, lemon juice, and ginger. Cover and refrigerate at least 1 hour or up to 2 days.

3. Toss arugula with mint and oil. Top with cranberry mixture. Makes 8 servings.

Sweet Potato and Hominy Stew

Posole, a hearty Mexican soup made with pork and hominy, is the inspiration for this hearty stew. Shown on page 121

WHAT YOU NEED

- 6 cloves garlic, minced
- 1 cup chopped onion
- 1 tablespoon olive oil
- 2 14-ounce cans reduced-sodium chicken broth
- 2 cups water
- 5 cups chopped, peeled sweet potatoes (3 medium)
- 1 tablespoon chili powder
- 1 teaspoon dried oregano, crushed
- 1 teaspoon ground cinnamon
- 1 teaspoon ground cumin
- 2 14.5- to 15.5-ounce cans golden hominy, rinsed and drained
- 1 large red sweet pepper, coarsely chopped
- 1 18-ounce tub refrigerated barbecue sauce with shredded pork
  Cilantro sprigs
  Lime wedges

WHAT YOU DO

1. In a large saucepan or Dutch oven cook garlic and onion in hot oil until tender. Stir in broth and the water; add sweet potatoes, chili powder, oregano, cinnamon, and cumin. Bring to boiling; reduce heat. Simmer, covered, 20 minutes. Stir in hominy, sweet pepper, and shredded pork. Cook and stir 5 minutes or until heated through.

2. Serve with cilantro and lime wedges. Makes 8 servings.

Soup Sticks

Shown on page 121

WHAT YOU NEED

- 1¼ cups warm water (105°F to 115°F)
- 1 package active dry yeast
- 3½ cups all-purpose flour
- ½ cup whole wheat flour
- ⅓ cup olive oil
- 1 egg
- ¼ cup packed brown sugar
- 2 teaspoons chili powder (optional)
- 1 teaspoon salt
- ½ teaspoon ground cinnamon
  Spicy Honey-Butter

WHAT YOU DO

1. In a mixing bowl combine warm water and yeast. Stir to dissolve. Add 1 cup of the all-purpose flour, the whole wheat flour, olive oil, egg, sugar, chili powder, salt, and cinnamon. Beat with electric mixer on low for 1 minute.
2. Stir in remaining flour to make soft dough that pulls away from sides of bowl (dough will be sticky). Coat a 2-quart container with *nonstick cooking spray*. Place dough in container. Cover and chill overnight in the refrigerator.
3. When ready to use, punch dough down. Turn out onto a floured sheet of parchment paper. Pat or roll dough into 15×12-inch rectangle. Transfer parchment with dough to a large baking sheet.
4. Using a floured pizza cutter or knife, cut dough widthwise into 20 strips about ¾ inch wide. (Dip cutter in flour as necessary to prevent sticking.) Cover; let rise 1 hour or until double in size. Brush with olive oil.
5. Preheat oven to 375°F. Bake for 20 minutes or until golden. Slide soup sticks onto cutting board; cool slightly.

Cut apart. Serve with Spicy Honey-Butter. Makes 20 sticks.
Spicy Honey-Butter: Whisk ¼ cup honey and ¼ teaspoon crushed red pepper into ½ cup (1 stick) softened butter.

Garlic-Herbed Bread

Shown on page 122

WHAT YOU NEED

- ½ cup butter, softened
- 2 tablespoons snipped fresh Italian parsley
- 1½ teaspoons minced garlic (about 3 cloves)
- ¾ teaspoon kosher salt or ½ teaspoon salt
  Dash black pepper
- 1 14- to 18-ounce baguette or Italian bread

WHAT YOU DO

1. Preheat oven to 375°F. In a small bowl combine butter, parsley, garlic, salt, and a dash of pepper.
2. Without cutting through bottom crust, slice baguette into 1½-inch slices. Generously spread butter mixture between slices. Wrap baguette in heavy foil. Bake for 15 minutes or until heated through. Serve warm. Makes 10 to 12 slices.

Spinach Salad with Brie Toast

For easy slicing, freeze wrapped Brie for 30 minutes before cutting. Shown on page 123

WHAT YOU NEED

- ⅔ cup fresh or frozen cranberries
- ¼ cup sugar
- ¼ cup white wine vinegar
- ¼ cup orange juice

- 2 teaspoons Dijon mustard
- ¾ cup olive oil
- 2 teaspoons finely snipped fresh sage
- ½ teaspoon salt
- ¼ teaspoon ground black pepper
- 16 ¼-inch slices baguette-style French bread, toasted*
- 8 ounces Brie cheese, cut into 16 wedges
- 10 cups packaged fresh baby spinach
- ½ cup dried cranberries
- ¼ cup pumpkin seeds (pepitas), toasted (optional)

WHAT YOU DO

1. Preheat broiler. For dressing, in a small saucepan combine fresh or frozen cranberries, sugar, and vinegar. Cook on medium heat about 5 minutes or until cranberries start to pop, stirring frequently. Cool.
2. Transfer cranberry mixture to a blender. Cover and blend until nearly smooth. Add orange juice and mustard; cover and blend until well mixed. With blender running, slowly add oil in a thin, steady stream. Continue blending until slightly thickened and creamy. Transfer to a small bowl. Whisk in sage, salt, and pepper. Set aside.
3. Place toasted bread slices on a baking sheet; top with cheese. Broil 5 to 6 inches from the heat for 1 to 2 minutes or until cheese melts.
4. In a serving bowl combine spinach, dried cranberries, and, if desired, pumpkin seeds. Pour ¾ cup of the dressing over spinach mixture; toss gently to coat. Serve salad with toast and additional dressing. Makes 8 servings.
*Test Kitchen Tip: To toast bread, place slices in a single layer on a baking sheet. Bake in a 350°F oven about 10 minutes or until golden brown.

Butternut Squash Bisque

Shown on page 123

WHAT YOU NEED

- 1 2½- to 3-pound butternut squash or three 12-ounce packages frozen cooked winter squash, thawed
- ¼ cup butter
- 1 medium onion, chopped
- 1 large carrot, coarsely chopped
- 1 stalk celery, coarsely chopped
- 2 cloves garlic, minced
- 2 large Braeburn or Gala apples, peeled, cored, and chopped
- 1 48-ounce box reduced-sodium chicken broth
- 1 cup apple cider or apple juice
- 2 canned chipotle peppers in adobo sauce, coarsely chopped
- ½ cup sour cream
- 3 ounces smoked Gouda or smoked cheddar cheese, finely shredded
       Crumbled cooked bacon, celery leaves, and/or shredded Gouda cheese (optional)

WHAT YOU DO

1. Peel, seed, and cube butternut squash. In a 6-quart Dutch oven melt butter on medium-high heat. Add fresh squash (if using), onion, carrot, celery, and garlic. Cook, stirring frequently, 10 minutes or until vegetables are tender. Add apples, broth, frozen squash (if using), cider, and chipotle peppers. Bring to boiling; reduce heat. Cover and simmer for 25 minutes or until vegetables and apples are tender. Remove from heat; cool slightly.

2. When slightly cooled, puree in pot using an immersion blender. (Or puree in batches in a blender; return soup to saucepan.) Blend in sour cream and heat

through. Remove from heat; stir in shredded Gouda until melted. If desired, top with bacon, celery leaves, and/or Gouda cheese. Makes 8 servings.

Peppermint-Fudge Pie

The combination of rich chocolate sauce, peppermint ice cream, and meringue makes this pie a dream come true for anyone craving the ultimate dessert indulgence. Shown on page 124

WHAT YOU NEED

     Chocolate Crumb Crust
- 1 cup sugar
- 1 5-ounce can (⅔ cup) evaporated milk
- 2 tablespoons butter
- 2 ounces unsweetened chocolate, cut up

A

- 1 teaspoon vanilla
- 2 pints (4 cups) peppermint ice cream
- ¾ cup sugar
- ½ cup boiling water
- ¼ cup meringue powder*
- 10 striped round peppermint candies, crushed (¼ cup)

WHAT YOU DO

1. Prepare Chocolate Crumb Crust. For fudge sauce, in a small saucepan combine the 1 cup sugar, the evaporated milk, butter, and chocolate. Cook and stir on medium heat until bubbly; reduce heat. Boil gently for 4 to 5 minutes or until mixture is thickened and reduced to 1½ cups, stirring occasionally. Remove from heat; stir in vanilla. If necessary, beat until smooth with wire whisk. Set aside to cool completely.

2. In a chilled bowl stir 1 pint of the peppermint ice cream until softened. Spread over cooled Chocolate Crumb Crust. Place the cooled fudge sauce in a pastry bag fitted with a round tip about ¼ inch in diameter. Pipe half the cooled fudge sauce over ice cream. Freeze about 2 hours or until nearly firm. Repeat with the remaining peppermint ice cream and the remaining fudge sauce. Return to freezer while preparing meringue.

3. For meringue, in a medium mixing bowl dissolve the ¾ cup sugar in the boiling water. Cool to room temperature.

B

Chocolate Loaf with Winter Fruit Glaze

Shown on page 124

Add the meringue powder. Beat on low until combined; beat on high until stiff peaks form (tips stand straight). Using a wooden spoon, fold 3 tablespoons of crushed candy into meringue. Spread meringue over pie, sealing to edge. Freeze about 6 hours or until firm.

4. Preheat oven to 475°F. Bake dessert for 3 to 4 minutes or just until meringue is light brown. Cover loosely with foil. Freeze for 6 to 24 hours before serving. Sprinkle with the remaining crushed candy before serving. Makes 12 servings.

Chocolate Crumb Crust: Preheat oven to 375°F. Lightly coat an 8-inch springform pan with nonstick cooking spray; set aside. In a medium bowl combine 1 cup very finely crushed vanilla wafers (about 22 cookies), ⅓ cup powdered sugar, and 3 tablespoons unsweetened cocoa powder. Stir in 3 tablespoons butter, melted. Pat crust mixture firmly into the bottom of the prepared pan. Bake for 7 to 8 minutes or until crust is firm. Cool in pan on a wire rack.

*Test Kitchen Tip: Meringue powder is a mixture of pasteurized dried egg whites, sugar, and edible gums. Look for it in the baking aisle of your supermarket or at a specialty food store.

Pumpkin-Pecan Tassies

These tiny treats contain all the tantalizing flavors of pumpkin and pecan pies. Shown on page 124

WHAT YOU NEED

- 1 15-ounce package rolled refrigerated unbaked piecrust (2 crusts)
- ¾ cup canned pumpkin
- ¼ cup granulated sugar
- 1 teaspoon pumpkin pie spice
- ⅛ teaspoon salt
- 1 egg, lightly beaten
- ¼ cup half-and-half, light cream, or milk
- ⅓ cup chopped pecans
- 1 tablespoon packed brown sugar
- 1 tablespoon butter, melted
  Maple syrup (optional)

WHAT YOU DO

1. Let piecrusts stand according to package directions. Preheat oven to 350°F. Unroll piecrusts. Use a 2½-inch round cookie cutter to cut 12 rounds from each piecrust. Gently ease pastry rounds into the bottoms and up sides of 24 ungreased 1¾-inch muffin cups; set aside.

2. For filling, in a large bowl stir together pumpkin, granulated sugar, pumpkin pie spice, and salt. Add egg; stir until combined. Gradually add half-and-half. Stir just until combined.

3. For pecan topping, stir together pecans, brown sugar, and melted butter.

4. Spoon about 2 teaspoons filling into each pastry-lined cup. Top each with a scant 1 teaspoon pecan topping. Bake about 30 minutes or until filling is set and crust is golden brown. Remove tassies from muffin cups and cool completely on a wire rack. If desired, drizzle tassies with maple syrup just before serving. Makes 24 tassies.

To Store: Place tassies in a single layer in an airtight container; cover. Store in the refrigerator up to 2 days or freeze up to 3 months; thaw about 1 hour at room temperature before serving.

WHAT YOU NEED

- 1 cup whipping cream
- 4 ounces semisweet chocolate, chopped
- ½ cup unsalted butter, softened
- 1 cup packed brown sugar
- 3 eggs
- 2 teaspoons vanilla
- 1½ cups all-purpose flour
- ¼ cup unsweetened cocoa powder
- 1 tablespoon baking powder
- ¼ teaspoon baking soda
  Winter Fruit Glaze

WHAT YOU DO

1. Preheat oven to 350°F. Butter and flour a 9×5×3-inch loaf pan; set aside.

2. In small saucepan heat whipping cream on medium heat just until hot. Remove from heat; add chocolate. Stir until chocolate is melted. Let cool.

3. Meanwhile, in a mixing bowl beat ½ cup butter with electric mixer on medium for 30 seconds. Add brown sugar; beat on high until fluffy, about 2 minutes, scraping bowl occasionally. Beat in eggs and vanilla. Beat in cooled chocolate mixture until smooth.

4. In a bowl stir together flour, cocoa, baking powder, and baking soda; add to butter mixture. Beat on medium until well combined. Pour batter in prepared pan; smooth with spatula.

5. Bake for 45 minutes or until toothpick inserted in center comes out clean. While loaf bakes, prepare Winter Fruit Glaze. Cool loaf in pan on rack for 10 minutes. Remove from pan; cool completely. Pour half of the Winter Fruit Glaze on loaf. Pass remaining glaze. Makes 8 servings.

Winter Fruit Glaze: In a skillet combine ½ cup brown sugar, 1 tablespoon lemon juice, 3 tablespoons water, and 3 tablespoons unsalted butter; cook and stir over medium heat until sugar is dissolved, about 1 minute. Stir in 2 tangerines, sliced and seeded, and ¼ cup cranberries. Cook, stirring frequently, about 3 minutes. Remove from heat.

*Create handmade ornaments and trims to share
with everyone who is near and dear to you.*

ornaments
on display

Bright ribbons crisscross to surround purchased ornaments making

Happy and Bright Trims, *above*. A pretty vintage button is glued to

the front of each trim. Sweet little cupcake liners stack up to make

Sugared Christmas Cups, *opposite*. Dip cupcake liners in meringue

powder, then into coarse sugar before stacking and filling them with

candy. Instructions are on page 138.

Tiny silver stars form constellations on a purchased silver ball to make a **Shooting Star Ornament**, *above left*. The stars are really little star stickers with trails of glitter glue. Brush on a little glue and add a dusting of glitter to make the elegant **Holly Leaf Trim**, *above right*. Instructions for both projects are on page 138.

Heavenly Angels, *above left*, are easy to make using wire in all shades of pink. Tiny gold bows are glued at the neck to complete the sweet little angels. Reminiscent of European vintage ornaments, this **Heirloom Bird Ornament,** *above right*, is painted with glass paint, sprinkled with glitter, and then embellished with colorful, tiny birds. Instructions and diagrams are on pages 139–140.

Create a **Jolly Old Elf Trim**, *above left*, from bits of paper and a little stuffing to make it come alive. This special Santa doubles as a package topper or a gift tag. Cut white paper into spirals to make a **Swirling Snowman Ornament**, *above right*. Clear crystal teardrops are made into **Sparkling Holiday Ornaments**, *opposite*, by simply adding a sprig of Christmas greenery, winter berries, and some bright red ribbon. Instructions are on pages 140–142.

Exchange purchased shiny balls for handmade and unbreakable trims.
Homespun Felted Trims, *above*, mimic classic Christmas ornament
shapes right up to the little caps on top. This trio is loosely knit in the
round, machine felted, and filled with soft fiberfill. Give personality
to each piece with needle felting, beads, or decorative stitches.

Instructions are on pages 142–143.

Create these one-of-a-kind **Star-Studded Ornaments**, *above* and *left*, using colorful felt, bits of ribbon, pearl-topped straight pins, and sequins. Instructions are on page 143.

Happy and Bright Trims
Shown on page 130

WHAT YOU NEED
FOR ONE ORNAMENT
Teardrop-shape ornament in bright color
10-inch length of 1-inch-wide
    bright-color ribbon
Crafts glue
Scissors
Fancy button with flat back

WHAT YOU DO
Be sure the ornament is clean and dry.
Wrap the ribbon around the ornament at
an angle. Glue in place, holding ribbon
in place if necessary until tacky. Trim
ends at an angle with scissors. Glue the
button to the front of the ornament
where the ribbon overlaps.

Sugared Christmas Cups
Shown on page 131

WHAT YOU NEED
FOR ONE ORNAMENT
3 cupcake liners: 2 red and 1 white
Meringue powder
Small bowl
Coarse white sugar
Small plate
Waxed paper
Spacers such as Pop Dots or small
    pieces of cardboard
Paper punch
8-inch piece of sheer ribbon
Lightweight peppermint candies

WHAT YOU DO
1. Mix the meringue powder according to
manufacturer's directions. Make enough
mixture to equal ¼ cup. Place in small
bowl. Place coarse white sugar on a small
plate. Dip each baking cup first into the
meringue mixture and then into the
sugar. Place on waxed paper to dry.
2. Place spacers between the cups and
stack. Use the paper punch to punch a
hole in each side. Knot the ribbon and
pull through from the outside. Thread the
ribbon inside and knot on the outside to
secure. Fill with candy.

Shooting Star Ornament
Shown on page 132

WHAT YOU NEED
Purchased round silver ornament
Silver sticker stars
Silver glitter glue
White star-print ribbon

WHAT YOU DO
Be sure the ornament is clean and dry.
Place the stickers on the bottom two-
thirds of the ornament. Use the glitter
glue to make star trails starting at the top
of the ornament and connecting to some
of the stars. Let dry. Tie the ribbon
through the top of the ornament.

Holly Leaf Trim
Shown on page 132

WHAT YOU NEED
Soft-green purchased ornament
Lightweight green paper
Crafts glue; scissors
Water
Paintbrush
Fine silver glitter (See Sources, *page 159*)

WHAT YOU DO
Be sure the ornament is clean and dry.
Cut small holly leaf shapes from the green
paper. In a small bowl, make a mixture of
⅔ glue and ⅓ water. Use the paintbrush
to brush the glue mixture on the back of
the holly leaf shapes. Lay the leaves at
the top of ornament. Brush the glue/water
mixture on leaf front. Immediately dust
with glitter. Brush the topper with the
mixture and dust with glitter. Allow to dry.

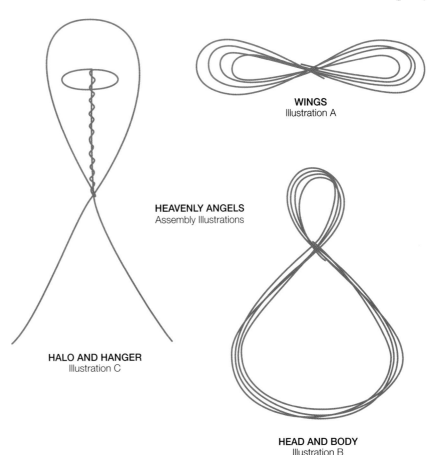

WINGS
Illustration A

HEAVENLY ANGELS
Assembly Illustrations

HALO AND HANGER
Illustration C

HEAD AND BODY
Illustration B

Heavenly Angels
Shown on page 133

WHAT YOU NEED
FOR ONE ANGEL
24-gauge wire, cut into the following
    lengths: 30 inches for wings,
    44 inches for head/body, 20 inches
    for halo and hanger
5 inches of ¼-inch-wide ribbon
Crafts glue
4 small round beads (optional)

WHAT YOU DO
For wings: Wrap the 30-inch length of
wire around four fingers 3 to 4 times to
form a loop. Twist in the middle. See
Illustration A. Set aside.

For head/body: Using the 44-inch piece
of wire, wrap around thumb and twist at
base to secure end (head). Wrap long
loose end in a continuous crazy eight
shape around 4 fingers to form the body.
Continue to loop over thumb (head) and
around the fingers (skirt) 3 times or until
the entire length of the wire is used. Twist
the end of the wire at the intersection of
the two shapes to secure the end. Use
fingers to mold and flatten out wire at the
base of the larger bottom section to make
skirt. See Illustration B. Set aside.

For halo and hanger: Using the 20-inch
piece of wire, about 4 inches from cut end,
form halo by wrapping wire loosely
around thumb to make a circle. Twist
wire at start of circle to finish halo and
continue twisting down the straight
4-inch tail that started this piece.

Loop long straight end up and over
halo in a circle to form hanger.
Twist at bottom. See Illustration C.

Attach 3 sections: Place the wings
behind the head/body section at the
twisted intersections. Hold the halo
piece behind the wings and body
sections. Take the remaining straight
wire from this halo piece and wrap
it around and over in a crisscross at
the intersection of both the wings
and the main body pieces, threading
the wire through the body and over
to the back around the wings, then
up through the body section again
several times, pulling tightly to
anchor the pieces together. Twist
the end at the back of the middle
intersection to complete. Decorate
the angel by tying a small bow and
gluing over the center intersection.
Glue small beads to halo, wings,
and/or body, if desired.

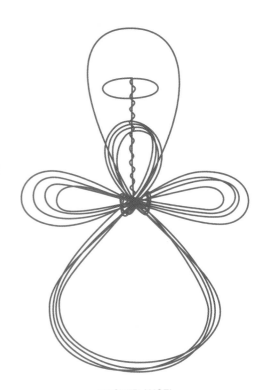

FINISHED ANGEL

Heirloom Bird Ornament

Shown on page 133

WHAT YOU NEED

Crafts glue; narrow white ribbon
Fine paintbrush; white glass paint
Fine white glitter
Purchased large light aqua ornament
Little bird and flower stickers

WHAT YOU DO

Run a line of glue around the center of the ornament. Glue ribbon atop glue and trim ends. Use white glass paint to paint a simple tree shape up from the ribbon line. Dust with glitter and allow to dry. Repeat on the other side. Place tiny birds and flowers on the branches. *Note:* Use little dots of glue under the stickers to hold if necessary.

Jolly Old Elf Trim

Shown on page 134

WHAT YOU NEED

Tracing paper; pencil; scissors
10-inch square of red lightweight
    cardstock
6-inch square of white lightweight
    cardstock
Scrap of cream lightweight cardstock
Scrap of green lightweight cardstock
Fine white glitter
Fine green glitter
Gold glitter glue
Fine-tip markers in red and charcoal
Paper punch; crafts glue
White tissue paper
Holly sticker
10-inch length of narrow red ribbon
Small jingle bell

WHAT YOU DO

1. Trace patterns, *opposite*, and cut out. Cut out chimney and hat from red; chimney top, beard, mustache, and hat trim from white; face from cream; and mittens from green. Use glitter glue to make brick marks on the red chimney front. Allow to dry.
2. Glue side and bottom of chimney together, leaving top open. Layer pieces to make Santa's hat and face. Use marking pens to make features. Spread glue on mittens and dust with green glitter. Allow to dry. Spread glue on hat trim, beard, and mustache and dust with white glitter. Allow to dry. Layer pieces to construct Santa, mittens, and chimney, then glue in place. Let dry.
3. Stuff tiny pieces of white tissue paper in chimney to add dimension. Punch hole in the top of the hat and thread a ribbon through the hole to hang. Glue a jingle bell to the top of the hat. Place a holly sticker on the chimney.

Swirling Snowman Ornament

Shown on page 134

WHAT YOU NEED

Tracing paper; pencil; scissors
White plain or printed lightweight
    cardstock
Scrap of red cardstock
White glitter glue
Red glitter glue; crafts glue
Black, gray, and orange fine-tip markers
Red chenille stem; paper punch
¼-inch-wide gold ribbon

WHAT YOU DO

1. Trace the patterns, *opposite* and *below*, and cut out. From white cardstock cut 2 of each body circle and 1 head circle.

Cut hat from red cardstock. Using the lines marked on the patterns, cut the swirls in all of the 4 body circles. Use white glitter glue to make swirls on one set of body circles. Use red glitter glue to outline the hat shape. Allow to dry. Draw face on the head circle using markers.
2. Place the large circles together, and secure at the top with a dot of glue. Repeat for the small set of body circles. Allow to dry.
3. Glue the head, middle circle, and bottom circles together, slightly overlapping circles. Glue the hat to the top of the head. Use a paper punch to make a hole in the top of the hat; thread ribbon through the hole for hanging. Wrap the chenille stem around the neck for a scarf.

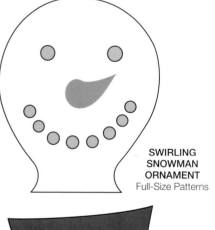

SWIRLING
SNOWMAN
ORNAMENT
Full-Size Patterns

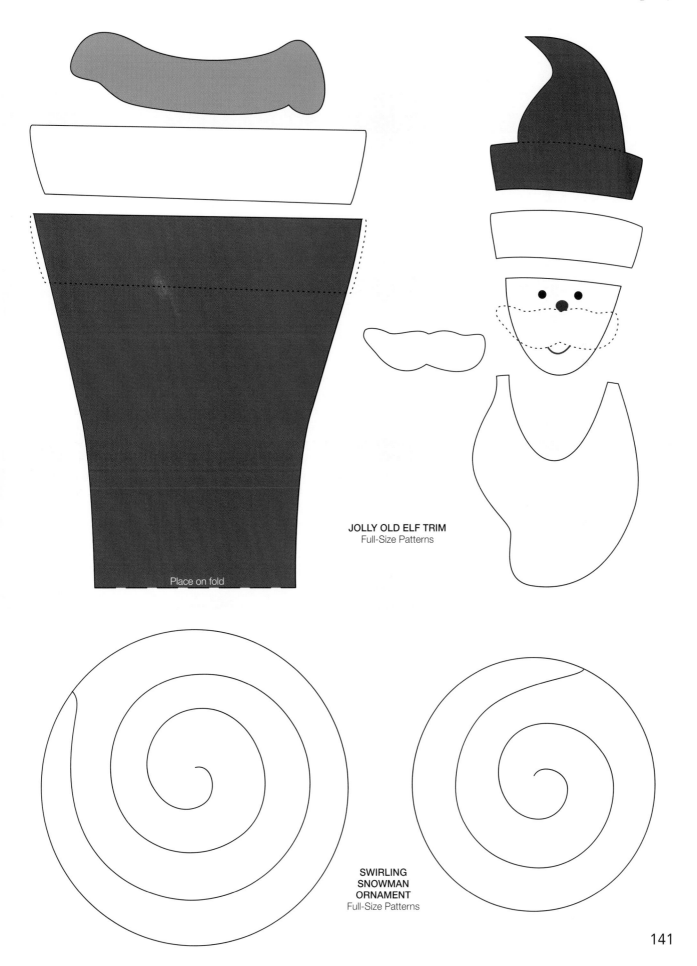

JOLLY OLD ELF TRIM
Full-Size Patterns

Place on fold

SWIRLING
SNOWMAN
ORNAMENT
Full-Size Patterns

Sparkling Holiday Ornaments
Shown on page 135

WHAT YOU NEED
Purchased crystal teardrop ornament
Artificial greenery and berries
1 yard of ¼-inch-wide red grosgrain
    ribbon
Hot glue and hot-glue gun

WHAT YOU DO
Wash the ornament and wipe with
window cleaner. Cut pieces of greenery
as desired. Make a small bow with half
of the ribbon. Hot-glue all of the pieces
on the top of the ornament. Thread the
remainder of the ribbon through the
top of the ornament.

Homespun Felted Trims
Shown on page 136

SKILL LEVEL: Intermediate

WHAT YOU NEED
Berroco Ultra Alpaca 100-percent-
    wool-blend worsted-weight yarn:
    Fennel (6249), Cardinal (6234),
    and Winter White (6201)*
Set of 4 double-pointed needles,
    Size 10½
Stitch marker or stitch pin
Needles: size 18/22 chenille, beading,
    and felting
Polyester fiberfill
T-pins; 18-gauge wire
Needle-nose pliers; toothbrush
Large and small green beads
Red 100-percent-wool roving
Acrylic felt: cream and green
Green embroidery floss

GAUGE: Knit ornaments so stitches are
loose and ornaments are large.

WHAT YOU DO
KNIT THE ORNAMENT BALLS
*Note: If you make yarn substitutions,
do not use machine-washable yarns.
They will not felt.*
Note: For abbreviations, see page 159.

Using the desired yarn color and one
dpn, loosely cast on 6 sts, leaving a
6-inch tail.
Row 1: *Inc 1*; rep from * to * to
end—12 sts.
Rnd 2: Divide sts onto 3 dpn, join, being
careful not to twist yarn, k around. Place
a stitch marker or pin at this point to
mark beg of rnd.
Rnd 3: *Inc 1, k1*; rep from * to * to
end of rnd—18 sts.
Rnd 4: Knit.
Rnd 5: *Inc 1, k2*; rep from * to * to
end of rnd—24 sts.
Rnd 6: Knit.
Rnd 7: *Inc 1, k3*; rep from * to * to
end of rnd—30 sts.
Rnds 8–12: Knit 5 rnds.
Rnd 13: *K3, k2tog*; rep from * to * to
end—24 sts.
Rnd 14: *K2, k2tog*; rep from * to * to
end—18 sts.
Rnd 15: *K1, k2tog*; rep from * to * to
end—12 sts.
Rnd 16: Knit.
Rnd 17: *K1, k2tog*; rep from * to * to
end—8 sts.
Rnd 18: K all sts onto 1 dpn.
Row 19: Purl.

Bind off all sts and tie off. Using the
6-inch tail, sew the bottom of the
ornament closed. Weave in loose ends.

MACHINE-FELT THE
ORNAMENT BALLS
Note: The dye in red yarns may bleed,
so machine-felt red ornaments separately.
Machine-felt cream ornaments in a
separate load. Machine-felt any other
color ornaments together in a different
load. If you knit the ornaments using
the suggested colors, you will need to
machine-felt each color separately.
For tips on felting, see *page 159*.
Note: The felted ornament should
measure approximately 3 to 3½ inches
from the bottom to the top of the neck.
Hand-rinse in cold water to remove
detergent. Wring and blot-dry ornaments
between towels. Stretch the ornaments
into shape. While ornaments are still wet,
firmly stuff them with fiberfill.

Using yarn and the yarn needle,
slip-stitch the sides of the neck together,
leaving the top open. Place on a wire
rack to air-dry.

KNIT THE ORNAMENT CAPS
Using a different color yarn and one dpn,
cast on 12 sts. Work the rows using just
two dpn or two straight needles.
Row 1: K1, *p2, k2*; rep from * to *,
end with p2, k1.
Row 2: P1, *k2, p2*; rep from * to *,
end with k2, p1.
Row 3: Rep Row 1.
Row 4: Rep Row 2.
Row 5: Work *p2tog*; rep from * to * to
end—6 sts.

Break yarn, leaving a 10-inch tail.
Starting at opposite end and using a yarn
needle, thread tail through remaining 6 sts;
tie off. Loosely sew seam; secure ends.

HAND-FELT THE
ORNAMENT CAPS
Wet the cap with hand soap or
dishwashing liquid and hot running tap
water. Rub the cap between your palms.
Alternate running the cap under hot
water and rubbing it. Add more soap as
needed. The felting is complete when the
piece fits the neck of the ornament ball.

Rinse the felted cap under cold water
to remove soap; blot it with a towel.
Shape cap on your middle finger,
making it boxlike. Place cap on neck
of ornament. Push a T-pin through top
to hold and flatten cap; let air-dry.
When dry, remove cap from ornament.

MAKE THE ORNAMENT HOOKS

Cut a 5-inch length of wire. Wrap one end twice around a dpn to knot the wire. Thread the wire through the center of the cap from the inside to the outside. Press the wire knot into the cap. Using the needle-nose pliers, create a coiled hook for hanging.

ASSEMBLE AND EMBELLISH ORNAMENTS

Note: For embroidery-stitch instructions, refer to the diagrams on *page 159.* Using long, evenly spaced whipstitches, sew the cap to the neck of the ornament.

Cream ornament: Work long blanket stitches around the neck of the ornament with the green yarn. Add a large bead to the end of each stitch using the beading needle and one strand of green embroidery floss.

Green ornament: Using tiny balls of roving, needle-felt dots on the ornament as follows: Place a tiny ball of roving on the ornament and then repeatedly poke the roving with the felting needle until the roving is secured to the ornament. Using a damp toothbrush, gently brush dots to smooth and blend them into the ornament. Add a small bead to the center of each dot using the beading needle and one strand of green embroidery floss.

Red ornament: Cut dime- and nickel-size circles and rings from cream and green felt. Using green floss, embroider the shapes onto the ornament using whipstitches, blanket stitches, and straight stitches.

Star-Studded Ornaments
Shown on page 137

WHAT YOU NEED

Tracing paper; pencil
4-inch plastic-foam balls
9×12-inch felt pieces in assorted colors
Boxes of ½-inch straight pins
Boxes of ½- and 1-inch pearl, gold, and colored-head corsage pins
Bags of ⅝-inch spoke sequins in silver, gold, and other assorted colors
Bags of 8- and 10-mm sequin cups in red, gold, silver, iridescent, turquoise, and green
Three 5-yard spools of holiday ribbon in ⅛-, ¼-, and ½-inch widths
3–5 yards of assorted silver and gold trims

Colored rickrack in ¼- and ⅝-inch widths
Scissors and pinking shears

WHAT YOU DO

1. Trace pattern, *below*, and cut out. Cut six pieces of felt in desired colors for each ball. Cover balls with felt, pinning in place. Secure pieces to the top and bottom of the ball with straight pins. Place pieces close together, align top and bottom edges, and pull each piece downward tightly to ensure the felt surface is smooth. Adjust pieces to fit the ball (narrow spaces between pieces can be covered later with ribbons) and pin piece edges to the ball. See Photo A.

2. Cut pieces of ribbon to cover where felt butts together and pin in place. See Photo B. Cut shapes such as stars if desired to pin on to ball. Decorate with corsage pins and sequins. See Photo C.

3. Layer at least three different sizes and colors of sequins and pin them to the ball with a straight or corsage pin. Stack smaller cup sequins over larger spoke sequins and place iridescent crystal sequins over colored sequins to create subtle chromatic shifts. Position stacked sequins close together to hide the felt beneath; fill in with cup sequins as needed. Cap each end with a large sequin and a pretty pin.

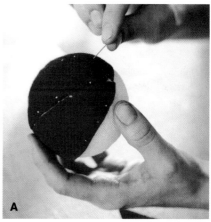

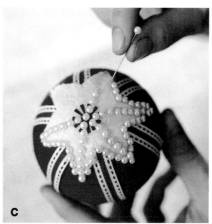

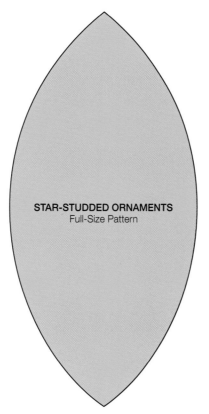

STAR-STUDDED ORNAMENTS
Full-Size Pattern

Share the joy of the season by making projects as a family to celebrate this special time of year.

a family affair

Embellish purchased cardboard letters with family photos to make a **Family Welcome Swag**, *opposite* and *above*. Letters in a variety of colors are decorated with small snapshots of family members, pieces of Christmas-print papers, and glitter glue to achieve a layered look. Use narrow ribbon to hold the letters together. For a quick variation, choose an initial for each person in the family to use as ornaments for a memorable holiday tree. Instructions are on page 152.

Your wee one will love his first Christmas when he gets to hold a **Sweet Baby Toy,** *above,* or **Gingerbread Twins,** *right.* All the little handmade toys are made using pinwale corduroy. Instructions and patterns are on pages 152–154.

Silver cookie cutters circle together to make a clever **Cookie Cutter Wreath**, *above left*. Add a pretty bow at the top of the wreath to match your holiday theme. As a family rediscover the meaning of the season by making a **Christmas Giving Jar**, *above right*. Choose a plain jar and decorate it with stickers and ribbon. Throughout the season, family members can put their extra change in the jar. On Christmas Eve place the jar on the doorstep of someone who could benefit from the generous gift. Instructions are on page 155.

Paper projects are fun family crafts. Try making a little forest of **Paper Christmas Trees**, *right*, or a **Mini Tree Garland**, *below*. The paper trees become 3-dimensional with a snip of the scissors. The garland is strung together using narrow ribbon. Instructions and patterns are on pages 155–156.

Let little ones help make these oh-so-sweet **Christmas Candy Kabobs**, *above*. Decorate favorite soft candies with bits of frosting and sugar and then thread them onto bamboo sticks. Instructions are on pages 156–157.

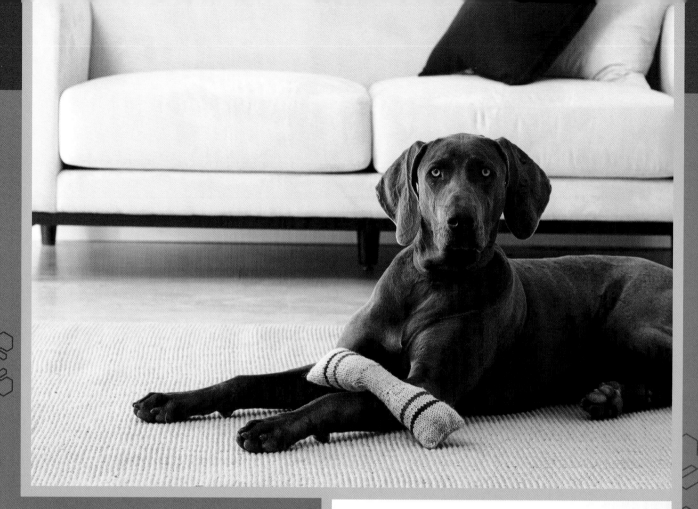

Every member of the family deserves a Christmas treat. This year knit a special **Doggie Bone Toy**, *above*, for your favorite Fido. Use cotton yarn and a little batting to make the toy chewable. Little kitties will love to play with their own knit and felted **Kitty Fish Toy**, *right*. Instructions and patterns are on pages 157–158.

Everyone in the family will want his or her own **Drawstring**

Backpack, *above*, made in personalized colors and patterns. These

cleverly designed backpacks have a zipper pocket in the front to hold

small books or treats, and the main compartment is big enough to

hold ballet shoes or even a soccer ball. Instructions are on page 158.

Instructions are on page 158.

Family Welcome Swag

Shown on pages 144, 145

WHAT YOU NEED
Fresh greenery swag
Cardboard letters in desired colors
    (available at crafts stores)
Scissors
Crafts glue
Scraps of printed scrapbook papers
Glitter glue to match papers
Small family photos
Narrow ribbon
Strong tape such as duct tape
Large bow in colors to match letters
Sprigs of berries (optional)

WHAT YOU DO
1. Decide which letters to use and lay them out in the order you decide. *Note:* Spell "family" or use surname if desired.

2. Cut small pieces of papers at an angle and glue on the letters. Glue photos on top of the papers. Outline with glitter glue. Make dots of glitter glue on open areas. Allow to dry. Lay the letters on the ribbon. Tape the ribbon to the back of the letters. Place the letters on the swag and tie in place. Add a bow at the top. Add sprigs of berries if desired.

Sweet Baby Toys
Shown on page 146

For Kitty and Bunny
WHAT YOU NEED
Tracing paper
Pencil
Scissors
Transfer paper
¼ yard *each* of blue (bunny) and green
    (kitty) pinwale corduroy
Straight pins
Permanent markers in blue and red
DMC cotton embroidery floss in
    appropriate colors
Embroidery needle; tweezers
Sewing thread to match fabrics
Needle
Polyester batting
½ yard of ¼-inch-wide lime green
    or blue ribbon

WHAT YOU DO
1. Trace patterns, *opposite*, onto tracing paper. Add another line ¼ inch all the way around to indicate the cutting line.

On a single layer of fabric (wrong side up) pin the transfer paper and trace image of character with details. Trace around cutting and sewing edges. Remove papers. Fold fabric double with right sides facing. Pin together. Cut out and remove pins.

2. With right side facing up on one fabric, place tracing of character to line up exactly with cut edge. Slip transfer paper between fabric and tracing. Trace all embroidery lines. Remove papers. Trace over any lines with permanent marker to clarify. Embroider all features using 3 strands of floss. *Note:* For embroidery stitch diagrams, *see page 159*. Place both sides of fabric together, pin in place (with wrong sides facing). Stitch on stitching line, leaving bottom of character open.

SWEET BABY TOYS
Kitty
Full-Size Pattern

SWEET BABY TOYS
Bunny
Full-Size Pattern

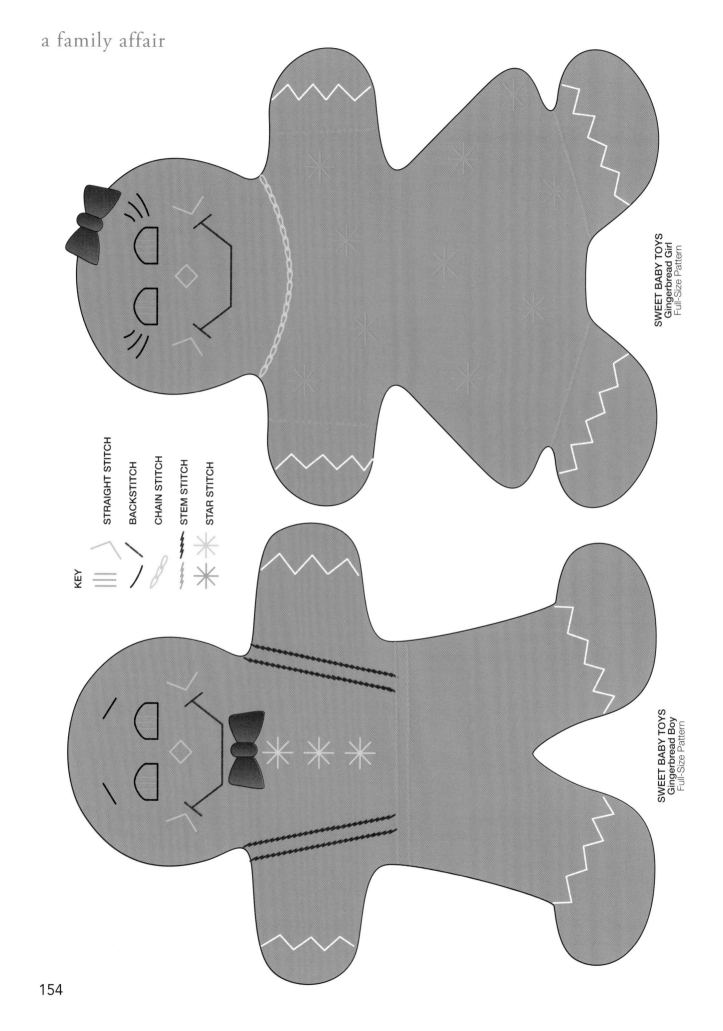

SWEET BABY TOYS
Gingerbread Girl
Full-Size Pattern

KEY

STRAIGHT STITCH

BACKSTITCH

CHAIN STITCH

STEM STITCH

STAR STITCH

SWEET BABY TOYS
Gingerbread Boy
Full-Size Pattern

3. Trim fabric, clip at corners, turn right side out. Use tweezers to insert stuffing in ears, arms, and legs. Blindstitch opening closed. Sew a length of ribbon on neck and form a bow with a separate piece of ribbon. Hand-stitch in place, stitching down entire ribbon and bow for safety. *Note: Always watch babies with baby toys.*

Gingerbread Twins
Shown on page 146

WHAT YOU NEED
Tracing paper; pencil
Fabric transfer paper
¼ yard pinwale brown corduroy fabric
Permanent markers
Embroidery floss in red, blue, gold, white, and tan
Matching sewing thread
Polyester batting
½ yard of ½-inch-wide red satin ribbon

WHAT YOU DO
Note: Stitches used are marked on patterns (stem outline stitches, backstitch, chain stitch, straight stitch).
1. Trace pattern of character, *opposite,* onto tracing paper. Add another line ¼ inch all the way around to indicate the cutting line. On a single layer of fabric (wrong side up) pin the transfer paper and trace image of character with details. Trace around cutting and sewing edges. Remove papers. Fold fabric double with right sides facing. Pin together. Cut out shapes and remove pins.
2. With right side facing up on one fabric, place tracing of character to line up exactly with cut edge. Slip transfer paper between fabric and tracing. Trace all embroidery lines. Remove papers. Go over any lines with permanent marker to clarify. Embroider all features using 3 strands of floss. *Note:* For embroidery stitch diagrams, see *page 159.* Place both sides of fabric together, pin in place (with wrong sides facing). Stitch on stitching line, leaving bottom of character open.
3. Trim fabric, clip at corners, turn right side out. Use tweezers to insert stuffing in arms and legs. Blindstitch opening closed. Sew a length of ribbon on neck and form a bow with a separate piece of ribbon. Hand-stitch in place, stitching down entire ribbon and bow for safety.

Cookie Cutter Wreath
Shown on page 147

WHAT YOU NEED
Metal cookie cutters
Crafts wire; wire cutters
Hot glue; hot-glue gun
2 yards 2-inch-wide ribbon

WHAT YOU DO
Arrange cutters in a circle and wire together using crafts wire. Twist a wire loop to the back for a hanger. Tie a bow and use hot glue to attach the bow at the top of the wreath.

Christmas Giving Jar
Shown on page 147

WHAT YOU NEED
Large jar with lid
Alphabet stickers
Motif stickers
Printed ribbon

WHAT YOU DO
Wash and dry the jar. Place the stickers on the jar front to spell "Christmas Jar." Press the motif stickers around the letters. Tie a ribbon around the lid. *Note:* Place extra change in the jar during the holiday season. On Christmas Eve, deliver the jar to a family in need or to a charity.

Paper Christmas Tree
Shown on page 148

WHAT YOU NEED
Tracing paper; pencil
Scissors
Crafts glue

Two 5×4-inch pieces of printed scrapbook paper or plain green paper
One 2-inch square of gold or yellow paper
Stick-on jewels or glitter glue

WHAT YOU DO
1. Trace the large tree pattern and star pattern, *page 156,* and cut out. Lay the tree pattern onto desired colors of green paper and draw around with a pencil. Make two trees, marking one with the slit at the top and one with the slit at the bottom. Cut out the tree shapes and cut the slits. Cut out the star from gold or yellow paper.
2. Lay the trees on a covered surface and decorate with jewels or glitter glue. Allow to dry. Slide the two trees together at slits. Adjust if necessary to make the tops meet. Add a drop of glue at the top to keep the points together if necessary. Glue the star at the top of the tree.

Mini Tree Garland
Shown on page 148

WHAT YOU NEED
Tracing paper; pencil
2×3-inch pieces of green print
   scrapbook paper
Narrow ribbon
Paper punch

WHAT YOU DO
Trace the pattern, *above right.*
Trace around pattern onto
printed paper pieces and
cut out. Punch holes in the
sides of the trees and string
the fine ribbon through
the holes.

MINI TREE
GARLAND
Full-Size Pattern

Tree 1 Slit

Tree 2 Slit

PAPER TREE
Full-Size Pattern
Cut 2

Christmas Candy Kabobs
Shown on page 149

WHAT YOU NEED
1 cup powdered sugar
1 tablespoon water
Small bowl
Jelly style candies such as Sunkist
Rolling pin; waxed paper
Bamboo skewers
Soft candy, such as gumdrops
Mini cutters
Colored sprinkles

WHAT YOU DO
1. Mix the powdered sugar and water
together in the small bowl. Set aside.
Place jelly candies between two pieces of
waxed paper and roll with the rolling pin.
See Photo A. Use the mini cutters to cut
out little shapes. See Photo B. Dip the
corners of the shape in the frosting
mixture or drizzle mixture on the shapes.
Add sprinkles if desired. See Photo C.
Let dry.
2. Place candies on the skewer in desired
order. See Photo D.
*Note: If making these with little children, be
careful that skewer doesn't poke little fingers.*

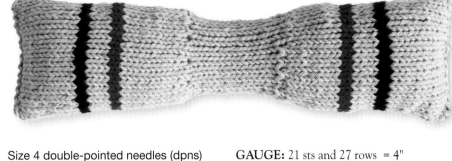

Doggie Bone Toy

Shown on page 150

SKILL LEVEL: Intermediate
FINISHED MEASUREMENTS:
Length = approx 10"
Circumference at widest part = approx 6½"

WHAT YOU NEED

Yarn such as Lion Brand Cotton (Art. 760)
100% cotton; 5 oz. (142 g); 236 yds.
(215 m); worsted weight
- 1 ball #186 Maize (A)
- 1 ball #153 Black (B)
- 1 ball #112 Poppy Red (C)

Size 4 double-pointed needles (dpns)
Stitch marker
Washable batting
Blunt-end yarn needle

Note: You'll need only a few yards
each of colors B and C for the stripes.
Omit B and C if you want to make a
solid-color toy.

GAUGE: 21 sts and 27 rows = 4"
(10 cm) in St st (knit all rounds).
TAKE TIME TO CHECK YOUR
GAUGE.

Note: Using small needles with worsted-
weight yarn keeps the batting from
showing through.

WHAT YOU DO

With A, cast on 30 sts. Divide evenly on
3 needles.
Rnd 1: Knit. Place marker at end of rnd.
Rep Rnd 1 for 12 rnds. Drop A.
Next 2 rnds: With B, knit. Drop B.
Next 4 rnds: With A, knit. Drop A.
Next 2 rnds: With C, knit. Drop C.
Next 10 rnds: With A, cont knitting in
St st for 10 rnds or until piece measures
desired length of wide end.
Dec rnd: With A, *k1, k2tog; rep from *
to end of rnd—20 sts. Cont knitting in St
st until middle section measures 3" or
desired length of middle section.
Inc rnd: *K2, M1 (see Make 1 directions,
page 66); rep from * to end of rnd—30
sts. Continue knitting in St st for 10 rnds
or to match length from the second stripe
to the center. Drop A.
Next 2 rnds: With C, knit. Drop C.
Next 4 rnds: With A, knit. Drop A.
Next 2 rnds: With B, knit. Drop B.
Next 13 rnds: With A, continue
knitting in St st for 13 rnds or until
section matches the length of the first
wide end. Remove marker. Bind off.

FINISHING
Sew one end tog. Cut and fold batting
into a roll to fit inside the knitted tube.
Add additional batting inside the wide
ends. Sew the other end tog.

A

B

C

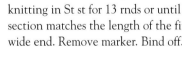

D

Kitty Fish Toy

Shown on page 150

SKILL LEVEL: Easy
FINISHED MEASUREMENTS:
Fish is approx 6" long after felting. Pom-poms are approx 1" in diameter.

WHAT YOU NEED

Yarn such as Lion Brand Wool (Art. 820) 100% wool; 3 oz. (85 g); 158 yds. (144 m); worsted weight
• 2 skeins #113 Scarlet
Size 11 knitting needles
Black cotton yarn for embroidery
Blunt-end tapestry needle
Tracing paper

WHAT YOU DO

Cast on 35 sts.

Knit skein of yarn in St st (knit 1 row, purl 1 row) for about 12", ending on WS. Bind off.

Felt fabric. *Note:* For felting instructions, see *page 159.* Let dry.

Trace full-size fish pattern, *below,* onto tracing paper; cut out. Pin pattern onto felted fabric twice, and cut out two fish. Stitch the fish together using a buttonhole stitch and black cotton yarn; embroider the eye with a French knot.

Make three small pom-poms and felt them. *Note:* For directions for making pom-poms, see *page 159.* String the pom-poms onto the cotton yarn and attach the yarn to the fish.

Drawstring Backpacks

Shown on page 151

WHAT YOU NEED FOR EACH BAG

½ yard canvas, twill, or other heavy-weight fabric
18×12-inch contrasting piece of fabric (for pocket section or top section)
18-inch zipper
4 yards of ⁹⁄₃₂-inch cable cord
Two ⅜-inch grommets (test to be sure two pieces of cord chosen will go through grommet opening)
Grommet installation tool
One package extra-wide double-fold bias tape
Thread to match fabrics

WHAT YOU DO

1. Cut two 18×9½-inch rectangles for pocket section. For back side of bag, cut one 18×20-inch piece. Cut one 11½×18-inch piece for the top of the bag front. Cut two 19×3-inch pieces for the top drawstring section. Cut two 5×5-inch squares for bottom reinforcements.
2. Fold the 5-inch squares in half to form triangles, wrong sides together. Place a triangle on each of the bottom corners on the right sides of each rectangle (one set on the bottom of one pocket section and one side on the bottom of the back bag piece). Pin in place with raw edges even and stitch close to diagonal folded edges. Baste around side and bottom edges.
3. Overcast across bottom of front 18-inch bag edge where pocket will join. Overcast top of both pocket pieces. Fold ½ inch to back side of both the top front section and top of pocket piece. Sew zipper to join these two pieces together, having colored teeth of zipper showing. Place back pocket section under top pocket section, having right side of bottom pocket to wrong side of top pocket piece and raw edges even. The back pocket

piece should be even with the top zipper tape edge. Pin in place along top zipper stitching line. Topstitch over top zipper stitching line again, through both layers of the pocket. Baste around side and bottom edges. On right side of pocket, stitch a line 7 inches from left side edge, from the bottom edge of the zipper down to the bottom edge of the pocket piece, stitching through both pocket layers to make a pocket for a water bottle.
4. Place right sides together and sew front to back, using ½-inch seam. Trim out fabric from square from seam allowance and trim corners. Finish seam allowances. Turn bag right side out; work bottom corners all the way out and press.
5. Hem the 3-inch edges of each of the 19×3-inch rectangles by turning under ½ inch twice. Topstitch in place. Fold each strip in half lengthwise with wrong sides together. Baste the long raw edge to form a tube.
6. Align the basted edges of the tube with the right side of the top raw edges of the body of the bag, placing the hemmed ends at the side seams and butting the ends of each tube to the other tube. Baste in place. Turn under one end of the bias tape to the inside at the end, enclose the seam allowance, and stitch the folded edge to the body of the bag. Topstitch near the seam line to reinforce the seam.
7. Place a grommet through the reinforced bottom corners of the bag, going through all layers, approximately 1 inch from the corner. Follow instructions with the grommet package. Split the cord in half, creating two equal pieces. Starting at one top end, place a cord through both tubes, coming out at the opposite end and through the grommet. Knot cord on back side of the bag. Repeat from the opposite end of the tube for the second cord. Adjust the cord lengths to fit comfortably when carrying the pack.

KITTY FISH TOY
Full-Size Pattern

Stitch Diagrams

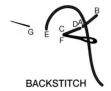

BACKSTITCH

CHAIN STITCH

FRENCH KNOT

RUNNING STITCH

STAR STITCH

STEM STITCH

STRAIGHT STITCH

Knitting Abbreviations

approx	approximately
beg	begin(ning)(s)
cn	cable needle
dec	decrease(s)(ing)
dpn(s)	double-pointed needle(s)
end	ending
est	established
inc	increase(s)(ing)
inc 1	increase 1 (knit into the front and back of the next stitch)
k or K	knit
k2tog	knit two stitches together (right-slanting decrease when right side facing)
p or P	purl
p2tog	purl two stitches together (right-slanting decrease when right side facing)
pat	pattern
pwise	as if to purl
rem	remain(s)(ing)
rep	repeat(s)(ing)
rev	reverse
rnd(s)	round(s)
RS	right side(s) of work
sl	slip
sl1-k	slip next stitch as if to knit
sl1-p	slip next stitch as if to purl
sm	slip marker
ssk	(slip, slip, knit) slip two stitches, one at a time knitwise, insert left needle and knit two together (left-slanting decrease when right side facing)
st(s)	stitch(es)
St st	stockinette stitch (knit RS rows, purl WS rows)
tbl	through the back loop(s)
tog	together
WS	wrong side(s) of work
yo	yarn over
yon	yarn over needle
yrn	yarn around needle
[ ]	work step in brackets the number of times indicated
( )	work instructions within parentheses in the place directed and the number of times indicated
*	repeat the instructions following the single asterisk as directed

Tips for Felting Wool

Felting wool fabric brings the fibers in the wool closer together and gives it a more compact look and feel. The texture becomes more irregular and interesting. Always choose 100% wool fabric to felt. Sweaters that are nearly 100% wool will work, but the fibers will not be as tight. Sweaters that have less than 90% wool will not work well.

Place the wool inside an old pillowcase to prevent any tiny fibers from washing out. Then wash the wool in very hot water with a little laundry detergent. Agitation of the wool loosens fibers and helps to shrink the wool. Dry the wool in a hot dryer to shrink the maximum amount.

Press the wool with a press cloth if desired. Tightly felted wool does not ravel, and edges and seams can usually be left raw or unfinished, similar to purchased felt.

Sources

Cookie Cutters
To order: 800-678-5752 or readershopping.com

Gingerbread Family
Ginger imps are exclusive designs and not available in stores. The 3 cutters range in size from 3–5 inches. Limited quantities. Item# CFHGimp $14.95

Snowflake Cutters
8-piece Let it Snow Collection Cutters range in size from 1.2–6 inches. Item# CFHsnow $12.95.

Vintage Cards and Stickers
The Gifted Line
johngrossmanline.com

Acorn Tops
braveink.com
Limited quantities

Paper/Scrapbooking Supplies
American Craft
americancrafts.com

Bazzill
bazzillbasics.com

General Crafting Supplies
Hobby Lobby
hobbylobby.com

Michaels
michaels.com
1-800-michaels

Designers

Judy Bailey, pages 9, 86, 90
Sue Banker, page 91
Mary Bruhn, page 73
Elizabeth Burnley, page 91
Galina Carrol, page 15
Carol Dahlstrom, pages 8, 12, 22, 59, 60, 61, 63, 64, 65, 70, 71, 72, 73, 74, 76, 77, 78, 79, 88, 89, 90, 92, 93, 95, 105, 110, 130, 131, 132, 133, 134, 135, 145, 146, 147, 148, 149
Mary Heaton, page 150
Heather Hill, page 64
Jeni Hilpipre-Wright, page 147
Marie Mayhew, page 94
Barbara Sestok, page 146
Margaret Sindelar, pages 36, 87
Jan Temeyer, pages 6, 8, 10, 11, 13, 37, 38, 39, 40, 41, 42, 43, 44, 45, 75, 87, 107, 108, 109, 111, 133, 146, 151

index